WORLD HISTORY

A JOURNEY THROUGH ANCIENT AND MEDIEVAL TEXTS

Revised First Edition

EDITED BY TOURAJ DARYAEE

UNIVERSITY OF CALIFORNIA, IRVINE

cognella
academic publishing

Bassim Hamadeh, CEO and Publisher
Michael Simpson, Vice President of Acquisitions
Jamie Giganti, Managing Editor
Jess Busch, Senior Graphic Designer
Marissa Applegate, Acquisitions Editor
Jessica Knott, Project Editor
Luiz Ferreira, Licensing Associate

First published in the United States of America in 2014 by Cognella, Inc.

ISBN: 978-1-62131-973-3

www.cognella.com   800-200-3908

CONTENTS

THE INDO-IRANIAN WORLD

GRECO-ROMAN WORLD

THE SILK ROAD CULTURES AND HISTORY FROM JAPAN TO ARMENIA TO EGYPT

ISLAMIC CIVILIZATION: ASIA AND AFRICA

MEDIEVAL PAGAN AND CHRISTIAN WORLD

ASIA: PHILOSOPHY, RELIGION AND THE STATE

INTRODUCTION

Historians are still searching for the best way to imagine and describe the history of humanity. This is a daunting task, as each one of us—based on our background, training and field of expertise—tend to have different notions of history and its turning points. However, in the past three decades the field of world history has steadily progressed, providing new means through which to understand the many different periods, empires, cultures and economic systems. Of course, we study history to understand who we are as humans, how we got here and why things are the way they are. The manner in which we can better understand what women and men of the past thought about themselves, their surroundings and the universe is to read their own writings from various periods in world history.

Naturally, one cannot possibly have records of every epoch and every location in the world, simply because not that much information has survived. Also, for the purposes of a world history course in an academic setting, one can similarly not include too many sources, as it becomes overburdening and tiresome. Hence, I have chosen a few sources which I believe will aid in a deeper understanding of the lives of people around the world from the third millennium BCE to the pre-modern period in Asia, Africa, America and Europe.

My reasoning in providing a small number of sources is that one can gain much from a single source if a professor or a teaching assistant evokes enough relevant questions relating to the assigned textbook and the lecture. In this way, the student can gain a deeper understanding of the subject matter and the complexity of human society and its relevance to our lives. I hope the students realize that the people's affairs and issues in the past were not very different from ours today, regardless of the technological advances in the past century which have made the world a very different place. Yet, we must not pass judgment on the ancients based on the standards and morals we hold today. The pre-modern Egyptians, Persians, Greeks, Romans and the Chinese were the product of their time and were bound by their geographical and cultural horizons. We simply should understand how they lived, operated and saw their world, and notice the processes that brought about the world that we live in today.

The way to use these sources is to first read the textbook, followed by the lectures, and then read the sources in this book associated with the regions and time periods under discussion. In addition to the explanations of the professor and the teaching assistant, nowadays a search on the Internet should give the student enough background to the text(s) in this world history reader. This search by the students themselves further encourages taking the first step in research, which in turn leaves a more indelible mark on one's mind than a simple explanation at the beginning of each source by the author. This is an extra step for the student, but a valuable mechanism for learning.

Touraj Daryaee
University of California, Irvine

CREATION ACCORDING TO THE YORUBA (WEST AFRICAN)

In the beginning was only the sky above, water and marshland below. The chief god Olorun ruled the sky, and the goddess Olokun ruled what was below. Obatala, another god, reflected upon this situation, then went to Olorun for permission to create dry land for all kinds of living creatures to inhabit. He was given permission, so he sought advice from Orunmila, oldest son of Olorun and the god of prophecy. He was told he would need a gold chain long enough to reach below, a snail's shell filled with sand, a white hen, a black cat, and a palm nut, all of which he was to carry in a bag. All the gods contributed what gold they had, and Orunmila supplied the articles for the bag. When all was ready, Obatala hung the chain from a corner of the sky, placed the bag over his shoulder, and started the downward climb. When he reached the end of the chain he saw he still had some distance to go. From above he heard Orunmila instruct him to pour the sand from the snail's shell, and to immediately release the white hen. He did as he was told, whereupon the hen landing on the sand began scratching and scattering it about. Wherever the sand landed it formed dry land, the bigger piles becoming hills and the smaller piles valleys. Obatala jumped to a hill and named the place Ife. The dry land now extended as far as he could see. He dug a hole, planted the palm nut, and saw it grow to maturity in a flash. The mature palm tree dropped more palm nuts on the ground, each of which grew immediately to maturity and repeated the process. Obatala settled down with the cat for company. Many months passed, and he grew bored with his routine. He decided to create beings like himself to keep him company. He dug into the sand and soon found clay with which to mold figures like himself and started on his task, but he soon grew tired and decided to take a break. He made wine from a nearby palm tree, and drank bowl after bowl. Not realizing he was drunk, Obatala returned to his task of fashioning the new beings; because of his condition he fashioned many imperfect figures. Without realizing this, he called out to Olorun to breathe life into his creatures. The next day he realized what he had done and swore never to drink again, and to take care of those who were deformed, thus becoming Protector of the Deformed. The new people built huts as Obatala had done and soon Ife prospered and became a city. All the other gods were happy with what Obatala had done, and visited the land often, except for Olokun, the ruler of all below the sky.

THE FIRST BOOK OF MOSES, CALLED GENESIS
THE HOLY BIBLE: KING JAMES VERSION

THE CREATION

1. In the beginning God created the heaven and the earth.
2. And the earth was without form, and void; and darkness was upon the face of the deep. And the Spirit of God moved upon the face of the waters.
3. And God said, Let there be light: and there was light.
4. And God saw the light, that it was good: and God divided the light from the darkness.
5. And God called the light Day, and the darkness he called Night. And the evening and the morning were the first day.
6. And God said, Let there be a firmament in the midst of the waters, and let it divide the waters from the waters.
7. And God made the firmament, and divided the waters which were under the firmament from the waters which were above the firmament: and it was so.
8. And God called the firmament Heaven. And the evening and the morning were the second day.
9. And God said, Let the waters under the heaven be gathered together unto one place, and let the dry land appear: and it was so.
10. And God called the dry land Earth; and the gathering together of the waters called he Seas: and God saw that it was good.

11. And God said, Let the earth bring forth grass, the herb yielding seed, and the fruit tree yielding fruit after his kind, whose seed is in itself, upon the earth: and it was so.
12. And the earth brought forth grass, and herb yielding seed after his kind, and the tree yielding fruit, whose seed was in itself, after his kind: and God saw that it was good.
13. And the evening and the morning were the third day.
14. And God said, Let there be lights in the firmament of the heaven to divide the day from the night; and let them be for signs, and for seasons, and for days, and years:
15. And let them be for lights in the firmament of the heaven to give light upon the earth: and it was so.
16. And God made two great lights; the greater light to rule the day, and the lesser light to rule the night: he made the stars also.
17. And God set them in the firmament of the heaven to give light upon the earth,
18. And to rule over the day and over the night, and to divide the light from the darkness: and God saw that it was good.
19. And the evening and the morning were the fourth day.
20. And God said, Let the waters bring forth abundantly the moving creature that hath life, and fowl that may fly above the earth in the open firmament of heaven.
21. And God created great whales, and every living creature that moveth, which the waters brought forth abundantly, after their kind, and every winged fowl after his kind: and God saw that it was good.
22. And God blessed them, saying, Be fruitful, and multiply, and fill the waters in the seas, and let fowl multiply in the earth.
23. And the evening and the morning were the fifth day.
24. And God said, Let the earth bring forth the living creature after his kind, cattle, and creeping thing, and beast of the earth after his kind: and it was so.
25. And God made the beast of the earth after his kind, and cattle after their kind, and every thing that creepeth upon the earth after his kind: and God saw that it was good.
26. And God said, Let us make man in our image, after our likeness: and let them have dominion over the fish of the sea, and over the fowl of the air, and over the cattle, and over all the earth, and over every creeping thing that creepeth upon the earth.
27. So God created man in his own image, in the image of God created he him; male and female created he them.
28. And God blessed them, and God said unto them, Be fruitful, and multiply, and replenish the earth, and subdue it: and have dominion over the fish of the sea, and over the fowl of the air, and over every living thing that moveth upon the earth.
29. And God said, Behold, I have given you every herb bearing seed, which is upon the face of all the earth, and every tree, in the which is the fruit of a tree yielding seed; to you it shall be for meat.

30. And to every beast of the earth, and to every fowl of the air, and to every thing that creepeth upon the earth, wherein there is life, I have given every green herb for meat: and it was so.
31. And God saw every thing that he had made, and, behold, it was very good. And the evening and the morning were the sixth day.

THE BUNDAHISHN (PRIMAL CREATION)

CHAPTER 1.

0. In the name of the Creator Ohrmazd.
1. The Zand-agahih ("Zand-knowing or tradition-informed"), which is first about Ohrmazd's original creation and the antagonism of the evil spirit, and afterwards about the nature of the creatures from the original creation till the end, which is the Future Existence (Tan-i Pasin).
2. As revealed by the religion of the Mazdayasnian (Zoroastrian or Mazda Worshiping Religion), so it is declared that Ohrmazd is supreme in omniscience and goodness, and unrivaled in splendor; the region of light is the place of Ohrmazd, which they call "endless light, and the omniscience and goodness of the unrivaled Ohrmazd is what they call "revelation.
3. Revelation is the explanation of both spirits together; one is he who is independent of unlimited time, because Ohrmazd and the region, religion, and time of Ohrmazd were and are and ever will be; while Ahriman (Evil Spirit) in darkness, with backward understanding and desire for destruction, was in the abyss, and it is he who will not be; and the place of that destruction, and also of that darkness, is what they call the "endlessly dark."
4. And between them was empty space, that is, what they call "air," in which is now their meeting.
5. Both are limited and unlimited spirits, for the supreme is that which they call endless light, and the abyss that which is endlessly dark, so that between them is a void,

and one is not connected with the other; and, again, both spirits are limited as to their own selves.

6. And, secondly, on account of the omniscience of Ohrmazd, both things are in the creation of Ohrmazd, the finite and the infinite; for this they know is that which is in the covenant of both spirits.

7. And, again, the complete sovereignty of the creatures of Ohrmazd is in the future existence, and that also is unlimited for ever and everlasting, and the creatures of Ahriman will perish at the time when the future existence occurs, and that also is eternity.

8. Ohrmazd, through omniscience, knew that Ahriman exists, and whatever he schemes he infuses with malice and greediness till the end; and because He accomplishes the end by many means, He also produced spiritually the creatures which were necessary for those means, and they remained three thousand years in a spiritual state, so that they were unthinking and unmoving, with intangible bodies.

9. The evil spirit, on account of backward knowledge, was not aware of the existence of Ohrmazd; and, afterwards, he arose from the abyss, and came in unto the light which he saw.

10. Desirous of destroying, and because of his malicious nature, he rushed in to destroy that light of Ohrmazd un-assailed by fiends, and he saw its bravery and glory were greater than his own; so he fled back to the gloomy darkness, and formed many demons and fiends; and the creatures of the destroyer arose for violence.

11. Ohrmazd, by whom the creatures of the evil spirit were seen, creatures terrible, corrupt, and bad, also considered them not commendable.

12. Afterwards, the evil spirit saw the creatures of Ohrmazd; there appeared many creatures of delight, inquiring creatures, and they seemed to him commendable, and he commended the creatures and creation of Ohrmazd.

13. Then Ohrmazd, with a knowledge of which way the end of the matter would be, went to meet the evil spirit, and proposed peace to him, and spoke thus: "Evil spirit! bring assistance unto my creatures, and offer praise! so that, in reward for it, ye (you and your creatures) may become immortal and undecaying, hungerless and thirstless."

14. And the evil spirit shouted thus: "I will not depart, I will not provide assistance for thy creatures, I will not offer praise among thy creatures, and I am not of the same opinion with thee as to good things. I will destroy thy creatures for ever and everlasting; moreover, I will force all thy creatures into disaffection to thee and affection for myself."

15. And the explanation thereof is this, that the evil spirit reflected in this manner, that Ohrmazd was helpless as regarded him, therefore He proffers peace; and he did not agree, but bore on even into conflict with Him.

16. And Ohrmazd spoke thus: "You are not omniscient and almighty, O evil spirit! so that it is not possible for thee to destroy me, and it is not possible for thee to force my creatures so that they will not return to my possession."

17. Then Ohrmazd, through omniscience, knew that: If I do not grant a period of contest, then it will be possible for him to act so that he may be able to cause the seduction of my creatures to himself. As even now there are many of the intermixture of mankind who practice wrong more than right.

18. And Ohrmazd spoke to the evil spirit thus: "Appoint a period so that the intermingling of the conflict may be for nine thousand years." For he knew that by appointing this period the evil spirit would be undone.

19. Then the Evil Spirit, unobservant and through ignorance, was content with that agreement; just like two men quarreling together, who propose a time thus: Let us appoint such-and-such a day for a fight.

20. Ohrmazd also knew this, through omniscience, that within these nine thousand years, for three thousand years everything proceeds by the will of Ohrmazd, three thousand years there is an intermingling of the wills of Ohrmazd and Ahriman, and the last three thousand years the evil spirit is disabled, and they keep the adversary away from the creatures.

21. Afterwards, Ohrmazd recited the Ahunwar (Zoroastrian prayer) thus: Yatha ahu vairyo ("as a heavenly lord is to be chosen"), &c. once, and uttered the twenty-one words; He also exhibited to the Evil Spirit His own triumph in the end, and the impotence of the evil spirit, the annihilation of the demons, and the resurrection and undisturbed future existence of the creatures for ever and everlasting.

22. And the evil spirit, who perceived his own impotence and the annihilation of the demons, became confounded, and fell back to the gloomy darkness; even so as is declared in revelation, that, when one of its (the Ahunwar's) three parts was uttered, the evil spirit contracted his body through fear, and when two parts of it were uttered he fell upon his knees, and when all of it was uttered he became confounded and impotent as to the harm he caused the creatures of Ohrmazd, and he remained three thousand years in confusion.

23. Ohrmazd created his creatures in the confusion of Ahriman; first he produced Vohuman ("Good Thought"), by whom the progress of the creatures of Ohrmazd was advanced.

24. The evil spirit first created Mitokht ("falsehood"), and then Akoman ("Evil Thought").

25. The first of Ohrmazd's creatures of the world was the sky, and his good thought (Vohuman), by good procedure, produced the light of the world, along with which was the good religion of the Mazdayasnians; this was because the Renovation of the World (Frashegird) which happens to the creatures was known to him!

26. Afterwards arose Ardwahisht, and then Shahrewar, and then Spandarmad, and then Hordad, and then Amurdad (These are Beneficent Spirits who aid Ohrmazd).
27. From the dark world of Ahriman were Akoman and Andar, and then Sovar, and then Nakahed, and then Tairev and Zairik (These are Evil Spirits who aid Ahirman).
28. Of Ohrmazd's creatures of the world, the first was the sky; the second, water; the third, earth; the fourth, plants; the fifth, animals; the sixth, mankind.

POPOL VUH

CHAPTER 1

This is the account of how all was in suspense, all calm, in silence; all motionless, still, and the expanse of the sky was empty.

This is the first account, the first narrative. There was neither man, nor animal, birds, fishes, crabs, trees, stones, caves, ravines, grasses, nor forests; there was only the sky.

The surface of the earth had not appeared. There was only the calm sea and the great expanse of the sky.

There was nothing brought together, nothing which could make a noise, nor anything which might move, or tremble, or could make noise in the sky.

There was nothing standing; only the calm water, the placid sea, alone and tranquil. Nothing existed.

There was only immobility and silence in the darkness, in the night. Only the Creator, the Maker, Tepeu, Gucumatz, the Forefathers,* were in the water surrounded with light. They were hidden under green and blue feathers, and were therefore called Gucumatz. By nature they were great sages and great thinkers. In this manner the sky existed and also the heart of E Alom, literally, those who conceive and give birth, E Qaholom, those who beget the children. In order to follow the conciseness of the text here the two terms are translated as the "Forefathers."

They were in the water because the Quiché associated the name Gucumatz with the liquid element. Bishop Núñiez de la Vega says that Gucumatz is a serpent with feathers,

---

The Popol Vuh: The Mythic and Heroic Sagas of the Kichés of Central America, trans. Lewis Spence. Copyright in the Public Domain.

which moves in the water. The Cakchiquel Manuscript says that one of the primitive peoples which migrated to Guatemala was called Gucumatz because their salvation was in the water.

Heaven, which is the name of God and thus He is called.

Then came the word. Tepeu and Gucumatz came together in the darkness, in the night, and Tepeu and Gucumatz talked together. They talked then, discussing and deliberating; they agreed, they united their words and their thoughts.

Then while they meditated, it became clear to them that when dawn would break, man must appear. Then they planned the creation, and the growth of the trees and the thickets and the birth of life and the creation of man. Thus it was arranged in the darkness and in the night by the Heart of Heaven who is called Huracán.

The first is called Caculhá Huracán. The second is Chipi Caculhá. The third is Raxa-Caculhá. And these three are the Heart of Heaven.

Then Tepeu and Gucumatz came together; then they conferred about life and light, what they would do so that there would be light and dawn, who it would be who would provide food and sustenance.

Thus let it be done! Let the emptiness be filled! Let the water recede and make a void, let the earth appear and become solid; let it be done. Thus they spoke. Let there be light, let there be dawn in the sky and on the earth! There shall be neither glory nor grandeur in our creation and formation until the human being is made, man is formed. So they spoke.

Then the earth was created by them. So it was, in truth, that they created the earth. Earth! they said, and instantly it was made.

Like the mist, like a cloud, and like a cloud of dust was the creation, when the mountains appeared from the water; and instantly the mountains grew.

Only by a miracle, only by magic art were the mountains and valleys formed; and instantly the groves of cypresses and pines put forth shoots together on the surface of the earth.

And thus Gucumatz was filled with joy, and exclaimed: "Your coming has been fruitful, Heart of Heaven; and you, Huracán, and you, Chipi-Caculhá, Raxa-Caculhá!"

"Our work, our creation shall be finished," they answered.

First the earth was formed, the mountains and the valleys; the currents of water were divided, the rivulets were running freely between the hills, and the water was separated when the high mountains appeared.

Thus was the earth created, when it was formed by the Heart of Heaven, the Heart of Earth, as they are called who first made it fruitful, when the sky was in suspense, and the earth was submerged in the water.

So it was that they made perfect the work, when they did it after thinking and meditating upon it.

THE EPIC OF GILGAMESH
SUMERIAN EPIC 2700 BCE

PROLOGUE

I will proclaim to the world the deeds of Gilgamesh. This was the man to whom all things were known; this was the king who knew the countries of the world. He was wise, he saw mysteries and knew secret things, he brought us a tale of the days before the flood, he went on a long journey, was weary, worn-out with labor, returning he rested, he engraved on a stone the whole story ...

When the gods created Gilgamesh they gave him a perfect body. Shamash the glorious sun endowed him with courage, the great gods made his beauty perfect, surpassing all others, terrifying like a great wild bull. Two thirds they made him god and one-third man.

In Uruk (city in Mesopotamia) he built walls, a great rampart, and the temple of blessed Eanna (belonging to god Anu and Goddess Ishtar) for the god of the firmament Anu, and for Ishtar the goddess of love. Look at it still today: the outer wall where the cornice runs, it shines with the brilliance of copper; and the inner wall, it has no equal. Touch the threshold, it is ancient.

TABLET I

Gilgamesh went abroad in the world, but he met with none who could withstand his arms till he came to Uruk. But the men of Uruk muttered in their houses, "Gilgamesh sounds the tocin for his amusement, his arrogance has no bounds by day or night. No son is left with his father, for Gilgamesh takes them all, even the children; yet the king should be a shepherd to his people. His lust leaves no virgin to her lover, neither the warrior's daughter nor the wife of the noble; yet this is the shepherd of the city, wise, comely, and resolute."

TABLET XI

You know the city of Shurrupak, it stands on the banks of Euphrates? That city grew old and the gods that were in it were old. There was Anu, lord of the firmament, their father, and warrior Enlil their counselor, Ninurta the helper, and Ennugi watcher over canals; and with them also was Ea. In those days the world teemed, the people plied, the world bellowed like a wild bull, and the great god was aroused by the clamor. Enlil heard the clamor and he said to the gods in council, "The uproar of mankind is intolerable and sleep is no longer possible by reason of the babel." So the gods agreed to exterminate mankind. Enlil did this, but Ea because of his oath warned me in a dream. He whispered their words to my house of reeds, "Reed-house, reed-house Wall, O wall, hearken reed-house, wall reflect; O man of Shurrupak, son of Ubara-Tutu; tear down your house and build a boat, abandon possessions and look for life despise worldly goods and save your soul alive. Tear down your house, I say, and build a boat. These are the measurements of the bark as your shall build her: let her beam equal her length, let her deck be roofed like the vault that covers the abyss; then take up into the boat the seed of all living creatures."

When I had understood I said to my lord, "Behold, what you have commanded I will honor and perform, but how shall I answer the people, the city, the elders?" Then Ea opened his mouth and said to me, his servant, "Tell them this: I have learnt that Enlil is wrathful against me, I dare no longer walk in his land nor live in his city: I will got down to the Gulf to dwell with Ea my Lord. But on you he will rain down abundance, rare fish and shy wild-fowl, a rich harvest-tide. In the evening the rider of the storm will bring you wheat in torrents." …

On the fifth day I laid the keel and the ribs, then I made fast the planking. The ground-space was one acre, each side of the deck measured one hundred and twenty cubits, making a square. I built six decks below, seven in all, I divided them into nine sections with bulk-heads between. … On the seventh day the boat was complete.

Then was the launching full of difficulty … I loaded into her … my family, my kin, the beast of the field both wild and tame, and all the craftsmen … In the evening, when the rider of the storm sends down the destroying rain, enter the boat and batten her down. The time was fulfilled, the evening came, the rider of the storm sent down the rain. I looked out at the weather and it was terrible, so I too boarded the boat and battened her down … With the first light of dawn a black cloud came from the horizon; it thundered within where Adad, lord of the storm was riding. In front over hill and plain Shullat and Hanish, heralds of the storm, led on. Then the gods of abyss rose up; Nergal pulled out the dams of the nether waters, Ninurta the war-lord threw down the dykes … A stupor of despair went up to heaven when the god of the storm turned daylight to darkness, when he smashed the land like a cup. One whole day the tempest raged, gathering fury as it went, it poured over the people like the tides of battle a man could not see his brother nor the people be seen from heaven.

For six days and six nights the winds blew, torrent and tempest and flood overwhelmed the world, and flood raged together like warring hosts. When the seventh day dawned the storm from the south subsided, the sea grew calm, the flood was stilled. I looked at the face of the world and there was silence, all mankind was turned to clay. The surface of the sea stretched as flat as a roof-top; I opened a hatch and the light fell on my face. Then I bowed low, I sat down and I wept, the tears streamed down my face, for on every side was the waste of water. I looked for land in vain, but fourteen leagues distant there appeared a mountain, and there the boat grounded; on the mountain of Nisir the boat held fast, she held fast and did not budge … When the seventh day dawned I loosed a dove and let her go. She flew away, but finding no resting-place she returned …

HAMMURABI LAW CODE

Hammurabi, the 6th king of Babylon, succeeded in uniting a splintered Babylonian kingdom probably in the first half of the 18th c. BCE (dates are disputed). His conquests extended from the kingdom of Larsa (in southern Mesopotamia) to Man (northern Mesopotamia).

Inscribed on this stele is the famous Law Code of Hammurabi, in Old Babylonian cuneiform. This detail shows the top part of the inscription, which spirals around the stele for nearly its entire height.

The relief at the top of the stele shows a simplified but standard type of "presentation scene" in which the king worshipfully approaches the divinity and in turn receives some kind of blessing. Here the standing King Hammurabi venerates Shamash, the Sun God (patron of justice), who is seated on his throne.

The stele was originally erected in Sippar, the city of the Sun God. It was carried off to Susa as booty, by the Elamites when they conquered Babylonia in the 12th c. BCE., where it was found by French excavators in the early 20th c. CE.

CODE OF HAMMURABI BABYLONIAN 1750 BCE

1. If any one accuses another, putting a ban upon him, but he can not prove it, then that (man) who accused him shall be put to death.

The Code of the Hammurabi, *Encyclopedia Britannica*, trans. L. W. King. Copyright in the Public Domain.

2. If any one bring an accusation against a man, and the accused go to the river and leap into the river, if he sink in the river his accuser shall take possession of his house. But if the river prove that the accused is not guilty, and he escape unhurt, then he who had brought the accusation shall be put to death, while he who leaped into the river shall take possession of the house that had belonged to his accuser.

3. If any one steals the property of a temple or of the court, he shall be put to death, and also the one who receives the stolen thing from him shall be put to death.

4. If any one steal cattle or sheep, or an ass, or a pig or a goat, if it belong to a god or to the court, the thief shall pay thirty-fold therefore; if they belonged to a freed man of the king he shall pay tenfold; if the thief has nothing with which to pay he shall be put to death.

5. If any one steals the minor son of another, he shall be put to death.

6. If any one takes a male or female slave of the court, or male or female slave of a freed man, outside the city gates, he shall be put to death.

7. If anyone receive into his house a runaway male or female slave of the court, or of a freedman, and does not bring it out at the public proclamation, the master of the house shall be put to death.

8. If any one find runaway male or female slaves in the open country and bring them to their masters, the master of the slaves shall pay him two shekels of silver.

9. If any one breaks a hole into the house, he shall be put to death before that hole and be buried.

10. If any one is committing a robbery and is caught, then he shall be put to death.

11. If the robber is not caught, then shall he who robbed claim under oath the amount of his loss; then shall the community compensate him for the goods stolen.

12. If persons are stolen, then shall the community pay one mina of silver to their relatives?

13. If any one be too lazy to keep his dam in proper condition, and does not so keep it; if then the dam break and all the fields be flooded, then shall he in whose dam the break occurred be sold for money, and the money shall replace the corn which he has caused to be ruined.

14. If he be not able to replace the corn, then he and his possessions shall be divided among the farmers who corn he has flooded.

15. If a tavern-keeper (female) does not accept corn according to gross weight in payment of drink, but takes money, and the price of the drink is less than that of the corn, she shall be convicted and thrown into the water.

16. If conspirators meet in the house of a tavern-keeper, and these conspirators are not captured and delivered to the court, the tavern-keeper shall be put to death.

17. If a "sister of a god" open a tavern, or enter a tavern to drink, then shall this woman be burned to death.

18. If any one "point the finger" at a sister of a god or the wife of any one, and can not prove it, this man shall be taken before the judges and his body shall be marked.

19. If a man take a woman to wife, but have no intercourse with her, this woman is not wife to him.

20. If a man's wife be surprised with another man, both shall be tied and thrown into the water, but the husband may pardon his wife and the king his slave.

21. If a man violate the wife of another man, who has never known a man, and still lives in her father's house, and sleep with her and be surprised, this man shall be put to death, but the wife is blameless.

22. If a man bring a charge against one's wife, but she is not surprised with another man, she must take an oath and then may return to her house.

23. If the "finger is pointed" at a man's wife about another man, but she is not caught sleeping with the other man, she shall jump into the river for her husband.

24. If a man wish to separate from a woman who has borne him children, then he shall give that wife her dowry, and a part of his land, garden, and property, so that she can rear her children.

25. If a man wishes to separate from his wife who has borne him no children, he shall give her the amount of her purchase money and the dowry she brought from her father's house, and let her go.

26. If a woman quarrel with her husband and say, "You are not congenial to me," the reasons for her prejudice must be presented. If she is guiltless, and there is no fault on her part, but he leaves and neglects her, then no guilt attaches to this woman, she shall take her dowry and go back to her father's house.

27. If she is not innocent, but leaves her husband, and ruins her house, neglecting her husband, this woman shall be cast into the water.

28. If a man take a wife and this woman giver her husband a maid-servant, and she bear him children, but this man wishes to take another wife, this shall be permitted to him; he shall not take a second wife.

29. If a man take a wife, and she bear him no children, and he intend to take another wife; if he take this second wife, and bring her into the house, this second wife shall not be allowed equality with his wife.

30. If a man be guilty of incest with his daughter, he shall be driven from the place.

31. If a man betroth a girl to his son, and his son have intercourse with her, but the father afterward defile her, and be surprised, then he shall be bound and cast into the water.

32. If a "sister of god," or prostitute, receive a gift from her father, and a deed in which it has been explicitly stated that she may dispose of it as she pleases, and give her complete disposition therof: if then her father die, then she may leave her property to whomsoever she pleases. Her brothers can raise no claim thereto.

33. If a father devote a temple-maid or temple-virgin to God and give her no present: if then the father die, she shall receive the third of a child's portion from the inheritance of her father's house, and enjoy its usufruct so long as she lives. Her estate belongs to her brothers.
34. If a son strike his father, his hands shall be cut off.
35. If a man put out the eye of another man, his eye shall be put out (an eye for an eye).
36. If he break another mans' bone, his bone shall be broken.
37. If he put out the eye of a freed man, or break the bone of a freed man, he shall pay one gold mina.
38. If he put out the eye of a man's slave, or break the bone of a man's slave, he shall pay one-half of its value.
39. If a man knock out the teeth of his equal, his teeth shall be knocked out.
40. If he knock out the teeth of a freed man, he shall pay one-third of a gold mina.
41. If any one strike the body of a man higher in rank than he, he shall receive sixty blows with an ox-whip in public.
42. If a freed man strike the body of another freed man, he shall pay ten shekels in money.
43. If the slave of a freed man strike the body of a freed man, his ear shall be cut off.
44. If a man strike a free-born woman so that she lose her unborn child, he shall pay ten shekels for her loss.
45. If the woman die, his daughter shall be put to death.
46. If a woman of free class lose her child by a blow, he shall pay five shekels in money.
47. If this woman dies, he shall pay half a mina.
48. If he strike the maid-servant of a man, and she lose her child, he shall pay two shekels in money.
49. If this maid-servant die, he shall pay one-third of a mina.
50. If a physician make a large incision with an operation knife and cure it, or if he open a tumor (over the eye) with an operating knife, and saves the eye, he shall receive ten shekels in money.
51. If the patient be a freed man, he receives five shekels.
52. If he be the slave of some one, his owner shall give the physician two shekels.
53. If a physician make a large incision with the operating knife, and kill him, or open a tumor with the operating knife, and cut out the eye, his hands shall be cut off.
54. If a physician make a large incision in the slave of a freed man, and kill him, he shall replace the slave with another slave.
55. If he had opened a tumor with the operating knife, and put out his eye, he shall pay half his value.
56. If a builder build a house for some one, and does not construct it properly, and the house which he built fall in and kill its owner, then that builder shall be put to death.
57. If it kill the son of the owner the son of that builder shall be put to death.

58. If it kill a slave of the owner, then he shall pay slave for slave to the owner of the house.

FEAST AT CALAH

This is the palace of Ashurnasirpal, the high priest of Ashur, chosen by Enlil and Ninurta, the favorite of Anu and of Dagan who is destruction personified among all the great gods—the legitimate king, the king of the world, the king of Assyria, son of Tukulti-Ninurta ... I took over again the city of Calah in that wisdom of mine, the knowledge which Ea, the king of the subterranean waters, has bestowed upon me, I removed the old hill of rubble; I dug down to the water level; I heaped up a new terrace ... I erected in Calah, the center of my overlordship, temples such as those of Enlil and Ninurta which did not exist before ...

When Ashurnasripal, king of Assyria, inaugurated the palace in Calah, a palace of joy and erected with great ingenuity, he invited into it Ashur, the great lord and the gods of his entire country, (he prepared a banquet of) 1,000 fattened head of cattle, 1000 calves, 10,000 stable sheep, 15,000 lambs—for my lady Ishtar along 200 head of cattle (and) 1000 sihhu-sheep—1000 spring lambs, 500 stags, 500 gazelles, 1000 ducks, 500 geese, 500 kurku-geese, 1000 mesuku-birds, 1000 qaribu-birds, 10,000 doves, 10,000 sukanunu-doves, 10,000 other assorted small birds, 10,000 assorted fish, 10,000 jerboa, 10,000 assorted eggs; 10,000 loaves of bread, 10,000 jars of beer, 10,000 skins with wine, ... 300 containers of pomegranates, 100 containers of grapes, 100 pistachio cones, 100 with fruits ...

When I inaugurated the palace at Calah, I treated for ten days with food and drink 47,074 persons, men and women, who were bid to come from across my entire country,

"The Banquet of Ashurnasipal II," *The Ancient Near East: A New Anthology of Texts and Pictures*, vol. 2, ed. James B. Pritchard, trans. A. Leo Oppenheim, pp. 99–104. Copyright © 1975 by Princeton University Press. Reprinted with permission.

also 5000 important persons, delegates from the country ..., also 16,000 inhabitants of Calah from all ways of life, 1500 official of all my palaces, altogether 69,574 invited guests from all the mentioned countries including the people of Calah; I furthermore provided them with means to clean and anoint themselves. I did them due honors and sent them back, healthy and happy, to their own countries.

GENESIS VI–VIII
OLD TESTAMENT (1000 BCE)

VI.5. The lord saw that the wickedness of man was great in the earth, and that every imagination of the thoughts of his heart was only evil continually. And the Lord was sorry that he had made man on the earth, and it grieved him to his heart. So the Lord said, "I will blot out man whom I have created from the face of the ground, man and beast and creeping things and birds of the air, for I am sorry that I have made them." But Noah found favor in the eyes of the Lord ...

VI.11. Now the earth was corrupt in God's sight, and the earth was filled with violence. And God saw the earth, and behold, it was corrupt ... And God said to Noah, "I have determined to make an end of all flesh; for the earth is filled with violence through them, I will destroy them with the earth. Make yourself an ark of gopher wood; make rooms in the ark, and cover it inside and out with pitch. This is how you are to make it: the length of the ark three hundred cubits, its breadth fifty cubits, and its height thirty cubits ... and set the door of the ark in its side; make it with lower, second, and third decks. For behold I will bring a flood of waters upon the earth, to destroy all flesh in which is the breath of life from under heaven; everything that is on the earth shall die. But I will establish my covenant with you; and you shall come into the ark, you, your sons, your wife, and your sons' wives with you. And of every living thing of all flesh, you shall bring two of every sort into the ark ... Also take with you every sort of food that is eaten ... Noah did this; he did all that God commanded him.

VII.6 Noah was six hundred years old when the flood of waters came upon the earth. And Noah and his sons and his wife and his son's wives with him went into the ark, to escape the waters of the flood … And after seven days the waters of the flood came upon the earth. (VII.11) On that day all the fountains of the great deep burst forth, and the windows of the heavens were opened. And rain fell upon the earth forty days and forty nights. (VII.17) The flood continued forty days upon the earth; and the waters increased, and bore up the ark, and it rose high above the earth.

VIII And God made a wind blow over the earth, and the waters subsided; the fountains of the deep and the windows of the heavens were closed, the rain from the heavens was restrained, and the waters receded from the earth continually. At the end of a hundred and fifty days the waters had abated and in the seventh month, on the seventeenth day of the month, the ark came to rest upon the mountains of Ararat (mountain in Anatolia). (VIII.6) At the end of the forty days Noah opened the window of the ark which he had made. Then he sent forth a dove from him, to see if the waters had subsided from the face of the ground; but the dove found no place to set her foot, and she returned to him to the ark.

PSALM 137

By the rivers of Babylon,
    There we sat down and wept,
    When we remembered Zion.

Upon the willows in the midst of it
    We hung our harps.

For there our captors demanded of us songs,
    And our tormentors mirth, saying,
    "sing us one of the songs of Zion."

How can we sing the LORD's song
    In a foreign land?

If I forget you, O Jerusalem,
    May my right hand forget her skill.

May my tongue cling to the roof of my mouth
    If I do not remember you,
    If I do not exalt Jerusalem
    Above my chief joy.

Remember, O LORD, against the sons of Edom
 The day of Jerusalem,
 Who said, "Raze it, raze it
 To its very foundation."

O daughter of Babylon, you devastated one,
 How blessed will be the one who repays you
 With the recompense with which you have repaid us.

How blessed will be the one who seizes and dashes your little ones
 Against the rock.

Egyptian Book of the Dead
Hymn to Osiris

Glory be to Osiris Un-nefer, the great god within Abydos, king of eternity, lord of the everlasting, who passeth through millions of years in his existence. Eldest son of the womb of Nut, engendered by Seb the Erpat (Chief of the Clan). lord of the crowns of the North and South, lord of the lofty white crown. As Prince of gods and of men he hath received the crook and the flail and the dignity of his divine fathers. Let thy heart which is in the mountain of Amenta be content, for thy son Horus is stablished upon thy throne. Thou art crowned lord of Tattu (identified with two towns in Lower Egypt: Busiris and Mendes) and ruler in Abtu. Through thee the world waxeth green in triumph before the might of Neb-er-tcher (A name of Osiris when his scattered limbs had been brought together and built up again into a body by Isis and Nephthys). He leadeth in his train that which is and that which is not yet, in his name Ta-her-seta-nef (The one who draws the world), he toweth along the earth in triumph in his name Seker (a form of the night sun). He is exceeding mighty and most terrible in his name Osiris. He endureth for ever and for ever in his name Un-nefer (A name of Osiris which means "the Good Being"). Homage to thee, king of kings, Lord of lords, Prince of princes, who from the womb of Nut hast possessed the world and hast ruled all lands and Akert (term for a necropolis). Thy body is of gold, thy head is of azure, and emerald light encircleth thee. O An (the Sun-god) of millions of years, all-pervading with thy body and beautiful in countenance in Ta-sert (A name of the underworld). Grant thou to the *ka* of Osiris, the scribe Ani, splendour in heaven and might upon earth and triumph in Neter-khert and that I may sail down to Tattu like a living soul and up to Abtu like a *bennu* (phoenix); and that I may go in and come out without repulse at the pylons of the Tuat. May there be given unto me loaves of bread in the house of coolness, and offerings of food in Annu, and a homestead for ever in Sekhet-Aru with wheat and barley.

"Hymn to Osiris," *The Book of the Dead*, trans. E. A. Wallace Budge. Copyright in the Public Domain.

EGYPTIAN POEM: NEW KINGDOM

"LOVE, HOW I'D LOVE TO SLIP DOWN TO THE POND"

Love, how I'd love to slip down to the pond, bathe with you close by on the bank.
Just for you I'd wear my new Memphis swimsuit, made of sheer linen, fit for a queen
Come see how it looks in the water!
Couldn't I coax you to wade in with me? Let the cool creep slowly around us?
Then I'd dive deep down and come up for you dripping.
Let you fill your eyes with the little red fish that I'd catch
And I'd say, standing there tall in the shallows:
Look at my fish, love, how it lies in my hand,
How my fingers caress it, slip down its sides …
But then I'd say softer, eyes bright with your seeing:
A gift of love. No words. Come closer and look, it's all me.

"Love, How I'd Love to Slip Down to the Pond," *Love Songs of the New Kingdom*, trans. John L. Foster, pp. 20.
Copyright © 1969 by University of Texas Press. Reprinted with permission.

THE HYMN TO ATON
NEW KINGDOM (AKHNATON PERIOD)

Praise of Re har-akhti, Rejoicing on the Horizon, in His Name as Shu Who is in the Aton-disc, living forever and ever; the living great Aton which is in jubilee, lord of all that the Aton encircles, lord of heaven, lord of earth, lord of the House of Aton in Akhet-Aton (Egyptian Capital at El-Amarna); and praise of the King of Upper and Lower Egypt, who lives on truth, the Lord of the Two Lands; nefer-kheperu-Re Wa-en-Re; the Son of Re, who lives on truth, the Lord of Diadems: Akh-en-Aton, long in his lifetime; and praise of the Chief Wife of the King, his beloved, the Lady of the Two Lands: Nefer-neferu-Aton Nefert-iti, living, healthy, and youthful forever and ever; by the Fan-Bearer on the Right Hand of the King ... Eye. He says:

When you set in the western horizon,
The land is in darkness, in the manner of death
They sleep in a room, with heads wrapped up,
Nor sees on eye the other.
All their goods which are under their heads might be stolen,
But they would not perceive it.
Every lion is come forth from his den;
All creeping things, they sting.
Darkness is a shroud, and the earth is in stillness.
For he who made them rests in his horizon (see Ps. 104:20–21)

At daybreak, when you arise on the horizon,
When you shine as the Aton by day,
Thou drive away the darkness and give your rays.
The Two lands are in festivity every day,
Awake and standing upon their feet,
For though has raised them up.
Washing their bodies, taking their clothing,
Their arms are (raised) in praise at thy appearance.
All the world, they do their work (Ps. 104.22–23).

HYMNS TO INDRA
VEDIC SANSKRIT 1500 BCE

INDRA HYMN

The chief wise god who as soon as born surpassed the gods in power; before whose vehemence the two worlds trembled by reason of the greatness of his valor: he, O men, is Indra.

Who made firm the quaking earth, who set at rest the agitated mountains; who measures out the air more widely, who supported heaven: he, O men, is Indra.

Who having slain the serpent released the seven streams, who drove out the cows by the unclosing of Vala, who between two rocks has produced fire, victor in battles: he, O men, is Indra.

By whom all things here have been made unstable, who has made subject the Dasa color and has made it disappear; who like a winning gambler the stake, has taken the possessions of the foe: he, O men, is Indra.

The terrible one of whom they ask "where is he," of whom they also say "he is not"; he diminishes the possessions of the niggard like the [player's] stake. Believe in him: he, O men, is Indra.

Who is furtherer of the rich, of the poor, of the suppliant Brahmin singer; who, fair-lipped is the helper of him that has pressed Soma and has set to work the stones: he, O men, is Indra.

In whose control are horses, kine, clans, all chariots; who creates the sun, the dawn; who is the guide of the waters: he, O men, is Indra.

The Rig Veda, trans. Ralph T. H. Griffith. Copyright in the Public Domain.

Whom the two battle-arrays, coming together, call upon divergently, both foes, the farther and the nearer; two having mounted the self-same chariot invoke him separately: he, O men, is Indra.

Without whom men do not conquer, whom they when fighting call on for help; who has been a match for every one, who moves the immovable: he, O men, is Indra.

Who slays with his arrow the unexpecting many that commit great sin; who forgives not the arrogant man his arrogance, who slays the Dasyu: he, O men, is Indra.

Who in the fortieth autumn found out Sambara dwelling in the mountains; who has slain the serpent as he showed his strength, the son of Danu, as he lay: he, O men is Indra.

The mighty seven-reined bull who let loose the seven streams to flow; who armed with the bolt spurned Rauhina as he scaled heaven: he, O men, is Indra.

Even Heaven and Earth bow down before him; before his vehemence even the mountains are afraid. Who is known as the Soma-drinker, holding the bolt is his arm, who holds the bolt in his hand: he, O men, is Indra.

Who with his aid helps him that presses Soma, him that bakes, him that offers praise, him that has prepared the sacrifice; whom prayer, whom Soma, whom this gift strengthens: he, O men, is Indra.

As he who, most fierce, enforced booty for him that presses and him that bakes, thou indeed art true. We ever dear to thee, O Indra, with strong sons, would utter divine worship.

HYMN TO PURUSHA
VEDIC SANSKRIT 1500 BCE

PURUSA

Thousand-headed was Purusa, thousand-eyes, thousand-footed. He having covered the earth on all sides, extended beyond it the length of ten fingers.

Purusa is this all, that has been and that will be. And he is the lord of immortality, which he grows beyond through food.

Such is his greatness, and more than that is Purusa. A fourth of him is all beings, three-fourths of him are what is immortal in heaven.

With three quarters Purusa rose upward; one quarter of him here came into being again. Thence he spread asunder in all directions to what eats and does not eat.

From him Viraj was born, from Viraj Purusa. When born he reached beyond the earth behind and also before.

When the gods performed a sacrifice with Purusa as an oblation, the spring was its melted butter, the summer its fuel, the autumn its oblation.

That Purusa, born in the beginning, they besprinkled as a sacrifice on the strew: with him the gods, the Sadhyas, and the seers sacrificed.

From that sacrifice completely offered was collected the clotted butter: he made that the beasts of the air, of the forest, and those of the village.

From that sacrifice completely offered were born the hymns and the chants; the meters were born from it; the sacrificial formula was born from it.

The Rig Veda, trans. Ralph T. H. Griffith. Copyright in the Public Domain.

From that arose horses and all such as have two rows of teeth. Cattle were born from that; from that were born goats and sheep.

When they divided Purusa, into how many parts did they dispose him? What [did] his mouth [become]? What are his two arms, his two thighs, his two feet called?

His mouth was the Brahman, his two arms were made the warrior, his two thighs the Vaisya; from his two feet the Sudra was born.

The moon was born from his mind; from his eye the sun was born; from his mouth Indra and Agni, from his breath Vayu was born.

THE AVESTAN HYMNS TO MITHRA

T his Yasht, one of the longest of the Avesta and one of the most interesting in a literary point of view, is not very instructive for mythology. It consists of long descriptive pieces, sometimes rather spirited, and of fervent prayers and invocations for mercy or protection. Originally Mithra was the god of the heavenly light (§§ 12, 50, 67, 104, 124 seq., 136 seq., etc.); and in that character he knows the truth, as he sees everything; he is therefore taken as a witness of truth, he is the preserver of oaths and good faith (§§ 2, 44 seq., 79 seq., 81 seq., etc.); he chastises those who break their promises and lie to Mithra, destroys their houses, and smites them in battle (§§ 17 seq., 28 seq., 35 seq., 47 seq., 99 seq., 105 seq., 112 seq., 128 seq., etc.).

Particularly interesting are §§ 115–118, as giving a sketch of moral hierarchy in Iran, and §§ 121–122, as being perhaps the source of the trials in the later Roman Mithraism. Cf. Vend. Intro. IV, 8 and *Ormazd et Ahriman*, §§ 59–61.

0. May Ahura Mazda be rejoiced!. …
Ashem Vohu: Holiness is the best of all good. …
I confess myself a worshipper of Mazda, a follower of
Zarathushtra, one who hates the Daevas, and obeys the laws of
Ahura;
For sacrifice, prayer, propitiation, and glorification unto [Havani],
the holy and master of holiness. …
Unto Mithra, the lord of wide pastures, who has a thousand ears,

ten thousand eyes, a Yazata invoked by his own name, and unto
Rama Hvastra,[1]
Be propitiation, with sacrifice, prayer, propitiation, and
glorification.
Yatha ahu vairyo: The will of the Lord is the law of holiness. …

I.

1. Ahura Mazda spake unto Spitama Zarathushtra, saying: "Verily, when I created Mithra, the lord of wide pastures, O Spitama! I created him as worthy of sacrifice, as worthy of prayer as myself, Ahura Mazda.[2]

2. "The ruffian who lies unto Mithra[3] brings death unto the whole country, injuring as much the faithful world as a hundred evil-doers[4] could do. Break not the contract, O Spitama! neither the one that thou hadst entered into with one of the unfaithful, nor the one that thou hadst entered into with one of the faithful who is one of thy own faith.[5] For Mithra stands for both the faithful and the unfaithful.

3. "Mithra, the lord of wide pastures, gives swiftness to the horses of those who lie not unto Mithra.
   "Fire, the son of Ahura Mazda, gives the straightest way to those who lie not unto Mithra.
   "The good, strong, beneficent Fravashis of the faithful give a virtuous offspring to those who lie not unto Mithra.

4. "For his brightness and glory, I will offer unto him a sacrifice worth being heard, namely, unto Mithra, the lord of wide pastures. "We offer up libations unto Mithra, the lord of wide pastures, who gives a happy dwelling and a good dwelling to the Aryan nations.

5. "May he come to us for help! May he come to us for ease! May he come to us for joy! May he come to us for mercy! May he come to us for health! May he come to us for victory! May he come to us for good conscience![6] May he come to us for bliss![7] he, the awful and overpowering, worthy of sacrifice and prayer, not to be deceived anywhere in the whole of the material world, Mithra, the lord of wide pastures.

6. "I will offer up libations unto him, the strong Yazata, the powerful Mithra, most beneficent to the creatures: I will apply unto him with charity[8] and prayers: I will offer up a sacrifice worth being heard unto him, Mithra, the lord of wide pastures, with the Haoma and meat, with the baresma, with the wisdom of the tongue, with the holy spells, with the speech, with the deeds, with the libations, and with the rightly-spoken words.
   "Yenhe hatam: All those beings of whom Ahura Mazda. …[9]

II.

7. "We sacrifice unto Mithra, the lord of wide pastures, who is truth-speaking, a chief in assemblies, with a thousand ears, well-shapen, with ten thousand eyes, high, with full knowledge,[10] strong, sleepless, and ever awake;[11]

8. "To whom the chiefs of nations offer up sacrifices, as they go to the field, against havocking hosts, against enemies coming in battle array, in the strife of conflicting nations.

9. "On whichever side he has been worshipped first in the fulness of faith of a devoted heart, to that side turns Mithra, the lord of wide pastures, with the fiend-smiting wind, with the cursing thought of the wise.[12]

"For his brightness and glory, I will offer him a sacrifice worth being heard. ...

III.

10. "We sacrifice unto Mithra, the lord of wide pastures, ... sleepless, and ever awake.

11. "Whom the horsemen worship on the back of their horses, begging swiftness for their teams, health for their own bodies, and that they may watch with full success those who hate them, smite down their foes, and destroy at one stroke their adversaries, their enemies, and those who hate them.[13]

"For his brightness and glory, I will offer him a sacrifice worth being heard. ...

IV.

12. "We sacrifice unto Mithra, the lord of wide pastures, ... sleepless, and ever awake;

13. "Who first of the heavenly gods reaches over the Hara[14], before the undying, swift-horsed sun[15]; who, foremost in a golden array, takes hold of the beautiful summits, and from thence looks over the abode of the Aryans with a beneficent eye.

14. "Where the valiant chiefs draw up their many troops in array;[16] where the high mountains, rich in pastures and waters, yield plenty to the cattle;[17] where the deep lakes, with salt waters, stand;[18] where wide-flowing rivers swell and hurry towards Ishkata and Pouruta, Mouru and Haroyu, the Gava-Sughdha and Hvairizem;[19]

15. "On Arezahi and Sawahi, on Fradadhafshu and Widadhafshu, on Wouru-bareshti and Wourujareshti, on this bright karshwar of Xwaniratha[20], the abode of cattle, the dwelling of cattle, the powerful Mithra looks with a health-bringing eye;

16. "He who moves along all the karshwars, a Yazata unseen, and brings glory; he who moves along all the karshwars, a Yazata unseen, and brings sovereignty; and increases[21] strength for victory to those who, with a pious intent, holily offer him libations.

"For his brightness and glory, I will offer him a sacrifice worth being heard. ...

V.

17. "We sacrifice unto Mithra, the lord of wide pastures, ... sleepless, and ever awake;
"Unto whom nobody must lie, neither the master of a house, nor the lord of a borough, nor the lord of a town, nor the lord of a province.

18. "If the master of a house lies unto him, or the lord of a borough, or the lord of a town, or the lord of a province, then comes Mithra, angry and offended, and he breaks asunder the house, the borough, the town, the province; and the masters of the houses, the lords of the boroughs, the lords of the towns, the lords of the provinces, and the foremost men of the provinces.

19. "On whatever side there is one who has lied unto Mithra, on that side Mithra stands forth, angry and offended, and his wrath[22] is slow to relent.[23]

20. "Those who lie unto Mithra, however swift they may be running, cannot overtake;[24] riding, cannot. ... ; driving, cannot. ... The spear that the foe of Mithra flings, darts backwards, for the number of the evil spells that the foe of Mithra works out.[25]

21. "And even though the spear be flung well, even though it reach the body, it makes no wound, for the number of the evil spells that the foe of Mithra works out.[26] The wind drives away the spear that the foe of Mithra flings, for the number of the evil spells that the foe of Mithra works out.

"For his brightness and glory, I will offer him a sacrifice worth being heard. ...

VI.

22. "We sacrifice unto Mithra, the lord of wide pastures, ... sleepless, and ever awake;
"Who takes out of distress the man who has not lied unto him, who takes him out of death.

23. "Take us out of distress, take us out of distresses, O Mithra! as we have not lied unto thee. Thou bringest down terror upon the bodies of the men who lie unto Mithra; thou takest away the strength from their arms, being angry and all-powerful; thou takest the swiftness from their feet, the eye-sight from their eyes, the hearing from their ears.

24. "Not the wound[27] of the well-sharpened spear or of the flying arrow reaches that man to whom Mithra comes for help with all the strength of his soul, he, of the ten thousand spies, the powerful, all-seeing, undeceivable Mithra.

"For his brightness and glory, I will offer him a sacrifice worth being heard. ...

VII.

25. "We sacrifice unto Mithra, the lord of wide pastures, ... sleepless, and ever awake;

"Who is lordly, deep, strong, and weal-giving; a chief in assemblies, pleased with prayers,[28] high, holily clever, the incarnate Word, a warrior with strong arms;

26. "Who breaks the skulls of the Daevas, and is most cruel in exacting pains; the punisher of the men who lie unto Mithra, the withstander of the Pairikas; who, when not deceived, establisheth nations in supreme strength; who, when not deceived, establisheth nations in supreme victory;

27. "Who confounds the ways of the nation that delights in havoc, who turns away their Glory,[29] takes away their strength for victory, blows them away helpless,[30] and delivers them unto ten thousand strokes; he, of the ten thousand spies, the powerful, all-seeing, undeceivable Mithra.

"For his brightness and glory, I will offer him a sacrifice worth being heard. ...

VIII.

28. "We sacrifice unto Mithra, the lord of wide pastures, ... sleepless, and ever awake;

"Who upholds the columns of the lofty house and makes its pillars[31] solid; who gives herds of oxen and male children to that house in which he has been satisfied; he breaks to pieces those in which he has been offended.

29. "Thou, O Mithra! art both bad and good to nations; thou, O Mithra! art both bad and good to men; thou, O Mithra! keepest in thy hands both peace and trouble for nations.

30. "Thou makest houses large, beautiful with women, beautiful with chariots, with well-laid foundations, and high above their groundwork;[33] thou makest that house lofty, beautiful with women, beautiful with chariots, with well-laid foundations, and high above its groundwork, of which the master, pious and holding libations in his hand, offers thee a sacrifice, in which thou art invoked by thy own name and with the proper words.

31. "With a sacrifice, in which thou art invoked by thy own name, with the proper words will I offer thee libations, O powerful Mithra!

"With a sacrifice, in which thou art invoked by thy own name, with the proper words will I offer thee libations, O most beneficent Mithra!

"With a sacrifice, in which thou art invoked by thy own name, with the proper words will I offer thee libations, O thou undeceivable Mithra!

32. "Listen unto our sacrifice,[34] O Mithra! Be thou pleased with our sacrifice, O Mithra! Come and sit at our sacrifice! Accept our libations! Accept them as they have been consecrated![35] Gather them together with love and lay them in the Garo-nmana![36].

33. "Grant us these boons which we beg of thee, O powerful god! in accordance[37] with the words of revelation, namely, riches, strength, and victory, good conscience and bliss,[38] good fame and a good soul; wisdom and the knowledge that gives happiness,[39] the victorious strength given by Ahura, the crushing Ascendant of Asha Vahishta, and conversation (with God) on the Holy Word.[40]

34. "Grant that we, in a good spirit and high spirit, exalted in joy and a good spirit, may smite all our foes; that we, in a good spirit and high spirit, exalted in joy and a good spirit, may smite all our enemies; that we, in a good spirit and high spirit, exalted in joy and a good spirit, may smite all the malice of Daevas and Men, of the Yatus and Pairikas, of the oppressors, the blind, and the deaf.[41] "For his brightness and glory, I will offer him a sacrifice worth being heard. …

IX.

35. "We sacrifice unto Mithra, the lord of wide pastures, . … sleepless, and ever awake; "Victory-making[42], army-governing, endowed with a thousand senses[43]; power-wielding, power-possessing, and all-knowing;

36. "Who sets the battle a going, who stands against (armies) in battle, who, standing against (armies) in battle, breaks asunder the lines arrayed. The wings of the columns gone to battle shake, and he throws terror upon the centre of the havocking host.

37. "He can bring and does bring down upon them distress and fear; he throws down the heads of those who lie to Mithra, he takes off the heads of those who lie unto Mithra.

38. "Sad is the abode, unpeopled with children, where abide men who lie unto Mithra, and, verily, the fiendish killer of faithful men. The grazing cow goes a sad straying way, driven along the vales[44] of the Mithradrujes: they[45] stand on the road, letting tears run over their chins[46].

39. "Their falcon-feathered arrows, shot from the string of the well-bent bow, fly towards the mark, and hit it not, as Mithra, the lord of wide pastures, angry, offended, and unsatisfied, comes and meets them.

"Their spears, well whetted and sharp, their long spears fly from their hands towards the mark, and hit it not, as Mithra, the lord of wide pastures, angry, offended, and unsatisfied, comes and meets them.

40. "Their swords, well thrust and striking at the heads of men, hit not the mark, as Mithra, the lord of wide pastures, angry, offended, and unsatisfied, comes and meets them.

"Their clubs, well falling and striking at the heads of men, hit not the mark, as Mithra, the lord of wide pastures, angry, offended, and unsatisfied, comes and meets them.

41. "Mithra strikes fear into them; Rashnu[47] strikes a counter-fear into them[48]; the holy Sraosha blows them away from every side towards the two Yazatas, the maintainers of the world.[49] They make the ranks of the army melt away, as Mithra, the lord of wide pastures, angry, offended, and unsatisfied, comes and meets them.[50]

42. "They cry unto Mithra, the lord of wide pastures, saying: "O Mithra, thou lord of wide pastures! here are our fiery horses taking us away, as they flee from Mithra; here are our sturdy arms cut to pieces by the sword, O Mithra!"

43. "And then Mithra, the lord of wide pastures, throws them to the ground, killing their fifties and their hundreds, their hundreds and their thousands, their thousands and their tens of thousands, their tens of thousands and their myriads of myriads; as Mithra, the lord of wide pastures, is angry and offended.

"For his brightness and glory, I will offer him a sacrifice worth being heard. …

X.

44. "We sacrifice unto Mithra, the lord of wide pastures, . … sleepless, and ever awake;

"Whose dwelling, wide as the earth, extends over the material world, large[51], unconfined[51], and bright, a far-and-wide-extending abode.

45. "Whose eight friends[52] sit as spies for Mithra, on all the heights, at all the watching-places, observing the man who lies unto Mithra, looking at those, remembering those who have lied unto Mithra, but guarding the ways of those whose life is sought by men who lie unto Mithra, and, verily, by the fiendish killers of faithful men.

46. "Helping and guarding, guarding behind and guarding in front, Mithra, the lord of wide pastures, proves an undeceivable spy and watcher for the man to whom he comes to help with all the strength of his soul, he of the ten thousand spies, the powerful, all-knowing, undeceivable god.

"For his brightness and glory, I will offer him a sacrifice worth being heard. …

XI.

47. "We sacrifice unto Mithra, the lord of wide pastures, ... sleepless, and ever awake; "A god of high renown and old age[53], whom wide-hoofed horses carry against havocking hosts, against enemies coming in battle array, in the strife of conflicting nations[54].

48. "And when Mithra drives along towards the havocking hosts, towards the enemies coming in battle array, in the strife of the conflicting nations, then he binds the hands of those who have lied unto Mithra, he confounds their eye-sight, he takes the hearing from their ears; they can no longer move their feet; they can no longer withstand those people, those foes, when Mithra, the lord of wide pastures, bears them ill-will.

"For his brightness and glory, I will offer him a sacrifice worth being heard. ...

XII.

49. "We sacrifice unto Mithra, the lord of wide pastures, ... sleepless, and ever awake;

50. "For whom the Maker, Ahura Mazda, has built up a dwelling on the Hara Berezaiti, the bright mountain around which the many (stars) revolve[55], where come neither night nor darkness, no cold wind and no hot wind, no deathful sickness, no uncleanness made by the Daevas, and the clouds cannot reach up unto the Haraiti Bareza[56];

51. "A dwelling that all the Amesha-Spentas, in one accord with the sun, made for him in the fulness of faith of a devoted heart, and he surveys the whole of the material world from the Haraiti Bareza.

52. "And when there rushes a wicked worker of evil, swiftly, with a swift step, Mithra, the lord of wide pastures, goes and yokes his horses to his chariot, along with the holy, powerful Sraosha and Nairyo-sangha,[57] who strikes a blow that smites the army, that smites the strength of the malicious.[58]

"For his brightness and glory, I will offer him a sacrifice worth being heard. ...

XIII.

53. "We sacrifice unto Mithra, the lord of wide pastures, ... sleepless, and ever awake;

54. "Who, with hands lifted up, ever cries unto Ahura Mazda, saying: "I am the kind keeper of all creatures, I am the kind maintainer of all creatures; yet men worship me not with a sacrifice in which I am invoked by my own name, as they worship the other gods with sacrifices in which they are invoked by their own names.

55. [59] "If men would worship me with a sacrifice in which I were invoked by my own name, as they worship the other Yazatas with sacrifices in which they are invoked by their own names, then I would come to the faithful at the appointed time; I would come in the appointed time of my beautiful, immortal life."

56. [60] "But the pious man, holding libations in his hands, does worship thee with a sacrifice, in which thou art invoked by thy own name, and with the proper words.

"With a sacrifice, in which thou art invoked by thy own name, with the proper words will I offer thee libations, O powerful Mithra!

"With a sacrifice, in which thou art invoked by thy own name, with the proper words will I offer thee libations, O most beneficent Mithra!

"With a sacrifice, in which thou art invoked by thy own name, with the proper words will I offer thee libations, O thou undeceivable Mithra!

57. "Listen unto our sacrifice, "O Mithra! Be thou pleased with our sacrifice, O Mithra! Come and sit at our sacrifice! Accept our libations! Accept them as they have been consecrated! Gather them together with love and lay them in the Garo-nmana [Garothman *i.e.* Heaven]!

58. "Grant us these boons which we beg of thee, O powerful god! in accordance with the words of revelation, namely, riches, strength, and victory, good conscience and bliss, good fame and a good soul; wisdom and the knowledge that gives happiness, the victorious strength given by Ahura, the crushing Ascendant of Asha-Vahishta, and conversation (with God) on the Holy Word.

59. "Grant that we, in a good spirit and high spirit, exalted in joy and a good spirit, may smite all our foes; that we, in a good spirit and high spirit, exalted in joy and a good spirit, may smite all our enemies; that we, in a good spirit and high spirit, exalted in joy and a good spirit, may smite all the malice of Daevas and Men, of the Yatus and Pairikas, of the oppressors, the blind, and the deaf.

"For his brightness and glory, I will offer him a sacrifice worth being heard. …

XIV.

60. "We sacrifice unto Mithra, the lord of wide pastures, . … sleepless, and ever awake;

"Whose renown is good, whose shape is good, whose glory is good; who has boons to give at his will, who has pasture-fields to give at his will; harmless to the tiller of the ground, [61] … beneficent; he, of the ten thousand spies, the powerful, all-knowing, undeceivable god.

"For his brightness and glory, I will offer him a sacrifice worth being heard. …

XV.

61. "We sacrifice unto Mithra, the lord of wide pastures, … sleepless, and ever awake;
    "Firm-legged[62], a watcher fully awake; valiant, a chief in assemblies; making the waters flow forward; listening to appeals; making the waters run and the plants grow up; ruling over the karshwars[63]; delivering[64]; happy[65]; undeceivable; endowed with many senses[66]; a creature of wisdom;

62. "Who gives neither strength nor vigour to him who has lied unto Mithra; who gives neither glory nor any boon to him who has lied unto Mithra.

63. "Thou takest away the strength from their arms, being angry and all-powerful; thou takest the swiftness from their feet, the eye-sight from their eyes, the hearing from their ears.
    "Not the wound of the well-sharpened spear or of the flying arrow reaches that man to whom Mithra comes for help with all the strength of his soul, he, of the ten-thousand spies, the powerful all-knowing, undeceivable god[67].
    "For his brightness and glory, I will offer him a sacrifice worth being heard. …

XVI.

64. "We sacrifice unto Mithra, the lord of wide pastures, … sleepless, and ever awake;
    "Who takes possession[68] of the beautiful, wide-expanding law, greatly and powerfully, and whose face looks over all the seven karshwars of the earth;

65. "Who is swift amongst the swift, liberal amongst the liberal, strong amongst the strong, a chief of assembly amongst the chiefs of assemblies; increase-giving, fatness-giving, cattle-giving, sovereignty-giving, son-giving, cheerfulness[69]-giving, and bliss[69]-giving.

66. "With whom proceed Ashi Vanguhi, and Parendi on her light chariot[70], the awful Manly Courage, the awful kingly Glory, the awful sovereign Sky, the awful cursing thought[71] of the wise, the awful Fravashis of the faithful, and he who keeps united together the many faithful worshippers of Mazda[72].
    "For his brightness and glory, I will offer him a sacrifice worth being heard. …

XVII.

67. "We sacrifice unto Mithra, the lord of wide pastures, . … sleepless, and ever awake;
    "Who drives along on his high-wheeled chariot, made of a heavenly[73] substance, from the Karshvare [keshwar] of Arezahi[74] to the Karshvare of Xwaniratha, the bright one; accompanied by[75] the wheel of sovereignty[76], the Glory made by Mazda, and the Victory made by Ahura;

68. "Whose chariot is embraced[77] by the great Ashi Vanguhi; to whom the Law of Mazda opens a way, that he may go easily; whom four heavenly steeds, white, shining, seen afar, beneficent, endowed with knowledge, swiftly[78] carry along the heavenly space[79], while the cursing thought of the wise pushes it forward;

69. "From whom all the Daevas unseen and the Varenya fiends[80] flee away in fear. Oh! may we never fall across the rush of the angry lord[81], who goes and rushes from a thousand sides against his foe, he, of the ten thousand spies, the powerful, all-knowing, undeceivable god.

"For his brightness and glory, I will offer him a sacrifice worth being heard. ...

XVIII.

70. "We sacrifice unto Mithra, the lord of wide pastures, ... sleepless, and ever awake;
"Before whom Verethraghna, made by Ahura, runs opposing the foes in the shape of a boar[82], a sharp-toothed he-boar, a sharp-jawed boar, that kills at one stroke, pursuing[83], wrathful, with a dripping face; strong, with iron feet, iron fore-paws[84], iron weapons, an iron tail, and iron jaws;

71. "Who, eagerly clinging to the fleeing foe, along with Manly Courage, smites the foe in battle, and does not think he has smitten him, nor does he consider it a blow till he has smitten away the marrow[85] and the column of life[86], the marrow[85] and the spring of existence.

72. "He cuts all the limbs to pieces, and mingles, together with the earth, the bones, hair, brains, and blood of the men who have lied unto Mithra[87].

"For his brightness and glory, we offer him a sacrifice worth being heard. ...

XIX.

73. "We sacrifice unto Mithra, the lord of wide pastures, ... sleepless, and ever awake;
"Who, with hands lifted up, rejoicing, cries out, speaking thus:

74. "'O Ahura Mazda, most beneficent spirit! Maker of the material world, thou Holy One!
"'If men would worship me[88] with a sacrifice in which I were invoked by my own name, as they worship the other gods with sacrifices in which they are invoked by their own names, then I should come to the faithful at the appointed time; I should come in the appointed time of my beautiful, immortal life[89].'"

75. "May we keep our field; may we never be exiles from our field, exiles from our house, exiles from our borough, exiles from our town, exiles from our country.

76. "Thou dashest in pieces the malice of the malicious, the malice of the men of malice: dash thou in pieces the killers of faithful men!

    "Thou hast good horses, thou hast a good chariot: thou art bringing help at every appeal, and art powerful.

77. "I will pray unto thee for help, with many consecrations, with good consecrations of libations; with many offerings, with good offerings of libations, that we, abiding in thee, may long inhabit a good abode, full of all the riches that can be wished for.

78. "Thou keepest those nations that tender a good worship to Mithra, the lord of wide pastures; thou dashest in pieces those that delight in havoc. Unto thee will I pray for help: may he come to us for help, the awful, most powerful Mithra, the worshipful and praiseworthy, the glorious lord of nations.

    "For his brightness and glory, I will offer him a sacrifice worth being heard. ...

XX.

79. "We sacrifice unto Mithra, the lord of wide pastures, ... sleepless, and ever awake;

    "Who made a dwelling for Rashnu[90], and to whom Rashnu gave all his soul for long friendship;

80. "Thou art a keeper and protector of the dwelling of those who lie not: thou art the maintainer of those who lie not. With thee hath Verethraghna, made by Ahura, contracted the best of all friendships[91], and thus it is how so many men who have lied unto Mithra, even privily[92], lie smitten down on the ground.

    "For his brightness and glory, I will offer him a sacrifice worth being heard. ...

XXI.

81. "We sacrifice unto Mithra, the lord of wide pastures, ... sleepless, and ever awake;

    "Who made a dwelling for Rashnu, and to whom Rashnu gave all his soul for long friendship;

82. "To whom Ahura Mazda gave a thousand senses[93] and ten thousand eyes to see. With those eyes and those senses, he watches the man who injures Mithra, the man who lies unto Mithra. Through those eyes and those senses, he is undeceivable, he, of the ten thousand spies, the powerful, all-knowing, undeceivable god.

    "For his brightness and glory, I will offer him a sacrifice worth being heard. ...

XXII.

83. "We sacrifice unto Mithra, the lord of wide pastures, ... sleepless, and ever awake;
    "Whom the lord of the country invokes for help, with hands uplifted;
    "Whom the lord of the town invokes for help, with hands uplifted;
84. "Whom the lord of the borough invokes for help, with hands uplifted;
    "Whom the master of the house invokes for help, with hands uplifted;
    "Whom the[94] ... in danger of death[95] invokes for help, with hands uplifted;
    "Whom the poor man, who follows the good law, when wronged and deprived
    of his rights, invokes for help, with hands uplifted.
85. "The voice of his wailing reaches up to the sky, it goes over the earth all around, it
    goes over the seven karshwars, whether he utters his prayer in a low tone of voice[96]
    or aloud.
86. "The cow driven astray invokes him for help[97], longing for the stables:
    ""When will that bull, Mithra, the lord of wide pastures, bring us back, and
    make us reach the stables? when will he turn us back to the right way from the
    den of the Druj where we were driven[98]?"
87. "And to him with whom Mithra, the lord of wide pastures, has been satisfied, he
    comes with help; and of him with whom Mithra, the lord of wide pastures, has
    been offended, he crushes down the house, the borough, the town, the province,
    the country.
    "For his brightness and glory, I will offer him a sacrifice worth being heard. ...

XXIII.

88. "We sacrifice unto Mithra, the lord of wide pastures, ... sleepless, and ever awake;
    "To whom the enlivening, healing, fair, lordly, golden-eyed Haoma offered up a
    sacrifice on the highest of the heights, on the Haraiti Bareza[99], he the undefiled
    to one undefiled, with undefiled baresma, undefiled libations, and undefiled
    words;
89. "Whom[100] the holy Ahura Mazda has established as a priest, quick in performing
    the sacrifice and loud in song. He performed the sacrifice with a loud voice, as a
    priest quick in sacrifice and loud in song, a priest to Ahura Mazda, a priest to the
    Amesha-Spentas. His voice reached up to the sky, went over the earth all around,
    went over the seven keshwars.
90. "Who first lifted up Haomas, in a mortar inlaid with stars and made of a heavenly
    substance. Ahura Mazda longed for him, the Amesha-Spentas longed for him, for the
    well-slapen body of him whom the swift-horsed sun awakes for prayer from afar[101].

91. "Hail to Mithra, the lord of wide pastures, who has a thousand ears and ten thousand eyes! Thou art worthy of sacrifice and prayer: mayest thou have sacrifice and prayer in the houses of men! Hail to the man who shall offer thee a sacrifice, with the holy wood in his hand, the baresma in his hand, the holy meat in his hand, the holy mortar in his hand[102], with his hands well-washed, with the mortar well-washed, with the bundles of baresma tied up, the Haoma uplifted, and the Ahuna Vairya sung through.

92. "The holy Ahura Mazda confessed that religion and so did Vohu-Mano, so did Asha-Vahishta, so did Khshathra-Vairya, so did Spenta-Armaiti, so did Haurvatat and Ameretat; and all the Amesha-Spentas longed for and confessed his religion. The kind Mazda conferred upon him the mastership of the world; and [so did they[103]] who saw thee amongst all creatures the right lord and master of the world, the best cleanser of these creatures.

93. "So mayest thou in both worlds, mayest thou keep us in both worlds, O Mithra, lord of wide pastures! both in this material world and in the world of the spirit, from the fiend of Death, from the fiend Aeshma[104], from the fiendish hordes, that lift up the spear of havoc, and from the onsets of Aeshma, wherein the evil-doing Aeshma rushes along with Vidotu[105], made by the Daevas.

94. "So mayest thou, O Mithra, lord of wide pastures! give swiftness to our teams, strength to our own bodies, and that we may watch with full success those who hate us, smite down our foes, and destroy at one stroke our adversaries, our enemies and those who hate us[106].
"For his brightness and glory, I will offer him a sacrifice worth being heard. ...

XXIV.

95. "We sacrifice unto Mithra, the lord of wide pastures, ... sleepless, and ever awake;
"Who goes over the earth, all her breadth over, after the setting of the sun[107], touches both ends of this wide, round earth, whose ends lie afar, and surveys everything that is between the earth and the heavens,

96. "Swinging in his hands a club with a hundred knots, a hundred edges, that rushes forwards and fells men down; a club cast out of red brass, of strong, golden brass; the strongest of all weapons, the most victorious of all weapons[108];

97. "From whom Angra Mainyu, who is all death, flees away in fear; from whom Aeshma, the evil-doing Peshotanu[109], flees away in fear; from whom the long-handed Bushyasta[110] flees away in fear; from whom all the Daevas unseen and the Varenya fiends flee away in fear[111].

98. "Oh! may we never fall across the rush of Mithra, the lord of wide pastures, when in anger[112]! May Mithra, the lord of wide pastures, never smite us in his anger; he who stands up upon this earth as the strongest of all gods, the most valiant of all gods,

the most energetic of all gods, the swiftest of all gods, the most fiend-smiting of all gods, he, Mithra, the lord of wide pastures[113]. "For his brightness and glory, I will offer him a sacrifice worth being heard. ...

XXV.

99. "We sacrifice unto Mithra, the lord of wide pastures, ... sleepless, and ever awake;
"From whom all the Daevas unseen and the Varenya fiends flee away in fear[114].
"The lord of nations, Mithra, the lord of wide pastures, drives forward at the right-hand side of this wide, round earth, whose ends lie afar.

100. "At his right hand drives the good, holy Sraosha; at his left hand drives the tall and strong Rashnu; on all sides around him drive the waters, the plants, and the Fravashis of the faithful.

101. "In his might, he ever brings to them falcon-feathered arrows, and, when diving, he himself comes there, where are nations, enemy to Mithra, he, first and foremost, strikes blows with his club on the horse and his rider; he throws fear and fright upon the horse and his rider.
"For his brightness and glory, I will offer him a sacrifice worth being heard. ...

XXVI.

102. "We sacrifice unto Mithra, the lord of wide pastures, ... sleepless, and ever awake;
"The warrior of the white horse, of the sharp spear, the long spear, the quick arrows; foreseeing and clever;

103. "Whom Ahura Mazda has established to maintain and look over all this moving[115] world, and who maintains and looks over all this moving world; who, never sleeping, wakefully guards the creation of Mazda; who, never sleeping, wakefully maintains the creation of Mazda;
"For his brightness and glory, I will offer him a sacrifice worth being heard. ...

XXVII.

104. "We sacrifice unto Mithra, the lord of wide pastures, ... sleepless, and ever awake;
"Whose long arms, strong with Mithra-strength, encompass what he seizes in the easternmost river and what he beats with the westernmost river, what is by the Sanaka of the Rangha and what is by the boundary of the earth.

105.   "And thou, O Mithra! encompassing all this around, do thou reach it, all over, with thy arms.

"The man without glory, led astray from the right way, grieves in his heart; the man without glory thinks thus in himself: "That careless Mithra does not see all the evil that is done, nor all the lies that are told."

106.   "But I think thus in my heart:

"'should the evil thoughts of the earthly man be a hundred times worse, they would not rise so high as the good thoughts of the heavenly Mithra;

"'should the evil words of the earthly man be a hundred times worse, they would not rise so high as the good words of the heavenly Mithra;

"'should the evil deeds of the earthly man be a hundred times worse, they would not rise so high as the good deeds of the heavenly Mithra;

107.   "'should the heavenly wisdom in the earthly man be a hundred times greater, it would not rise so high as the heavenly w'isdom in the heavenly Mithra;

"And thus, should the ears of the earthly man hear a hundred time better, he would not hear so well as the heavenly Mithra, whose ear hears well who has a thousand senses, and sees every man that tells a lie."

"Mithra stands up in his strength, he drives in the awfulness of royalty, and sends from his eyes beautiful looks that shine from afar, (saying):

108.   "Who will offer me a sacrifice? Who will lie unto me? Who thinks me a god worthy of a good sacrifice? Who thinks me worthy only of a bad sacrifice? To whom shall I, in my might, impart brightness and glory? To whom bodily health? To whom shall I, in my might, impart riches and full weal? Whom shall I bless by raising him a virtuous offspring?

109.   "'To whom shall I give in return, without his thinking of it, the awful sovereignty, beautifully arrayed, with many armies, and most perfect; the sovereignty of an all-powerful tyrant, who fells down heads, valiant, smiting, and unsmitten; who orders chastisement to be done and his order is done at once, which he has ordered in his anger?"

"O Mithra! when thou art offended and not satisfied, he soothes thy mind, and makes Mithra satisfied.

110.   "'To whom shall I, in my might, impart sickness and death? To whom shall I impart poverty and sterility? Of whom shall I at one stroke cut off the offspring!

111.   "'From whom shall I take away, without his thinking of it, the awful sovereignty, beautifully arrayed, with many armies, and most perfect; the sovereignty of an all-powerful tyrant, who fells down heads, valiant, smiting, and unsmitten; who orders chastisement to be done and his order is done at once, which he has ordered in his anger."

"O Mithra! while thou art satisfied and not angry, he moves thy heart to anger, and makes Mithra unsatisfied. "For his brightness and glory, I will offer him a sacrifice worth being heard. ...

XXVIII.

112. "We sacrifice unto Mithra, the lord of wide pastures, ... sleepless, and ever awake;
"A warrior with a silver helm, a golden cuirass, who kills with the poniard, strong, valiant, lord of the borough. Bright are the ways of Mithra, by which he goes towards the country, when, wishing well, he turns its plains and vales to pasture grounds,

113. "And then cattle and males come to graze, as many as he wants.
"May Mithra and Ahura, the high gods, come to us for help, when the poniard lifts up its voice aloud, when the nostrils of the horses quiver, when the poniards, ... when the strings of the bows whistle and shoot sharp arrows; then the brood of those whose libations are hated fall smitten to the ground, with their hair torn off.

114. "So mayest thou, O Mithra, lord of wide pastures! give swiftness to our teams, strength to our own bodies, and that we may watch with full success those who hate us, smite down our foes, and destroy at one stroke our adversaries, our enemies, and those who hate us.
"For his brightness and glory, I will offer him a sacrifice worth being heard. ...

XXIX.

115. "We sacrifice unto Mithra, the lord of wide pastures, ... sleepless, and ever awake.
"O Mithra, lord of wide pastures! thou master of the house, of the borough, of the town, of the country, thou Zarathushtrotema!

116. "Mithra is twentyfold between two friends or two relations; "Mithra is thirtyfold between two men of the same group; "Mithra is fortyfold between two partners;
"Mithra is fiftyfold between wife and husband;
"Mithra is sixtyfold between two pupils (of the same master);
"Mithra is seventyfold between the pupil and his master;
"Mithra is eightyfold between the son-in-law and his father-in-law;
"Mithra is ninetyfold between two brothers;

117. "Mithra is a hundredfold between the father and the son; "Mithra is a thousand-fold between two nations;
"Mithra is ten thousandfold when connected with the Law of Mazda, and then he will be every day of victorious strength.

118. "May I come unto thee with a prayer that goes lowly or goes highly! As this sun rises up above the Hara Berezaiti and then fulfils its career, so may I, O Spitama! with a prayer that goes lowly or goes highly, rise up above the will of the fiend Angra Mainyu!
"For his brightness and glory, I will offer him a sacrifice worth being heard. …

XXX.

119. "We sacrifice unto Mithra, the lord of wide pastwes … sleepless, and ever awake,
"Offer up a sacrifice unto Mithra, O Spitama! and order thy pupils to do the same.
"Let the worshipper of Mazda sacrifice unto thee with small cattle, with black cattle, with flying birds, gliding forward on wings.

120. "To Mithra all the faithful worshipers of Mazda must give strength and energy with offered and proffered Haomas, which the Zaotar proffers unto him and gives in sacrifice. Let the faithful man drink of the libations cleanly prepared, which if he does, if he offers them unto Mithra, the lord of wide pastures, Mithra will be pleased with him and without anger."

121. Zarathushtra asked him: "O Ahura Mazda! how shall the faithful man drink the libations cleanly prepared, which if he does and he offers them unto Mithra, the lord of wide pastures, Mithra will be pleased with him and without anger?"

122. Ahura Mazda answered: "Let them wash their bodies three days and three nights; let them undergo thirty strokes for the sacrifice and prayer unto Mithra, the lord of wide pastures. Let them wash their bodies two days and two nights; let them undergo twenty strokes for the sacrifice and prayer unto Mithra, the lord of wide pastures. Let no man drink of these libations who does not know the staota yesnya: Vispe ratavo.
"For his brightness and glory, I will offer him a sacrifice worth being heard. …

XXXI.

123. "We sacrifice unto Mithra, the lord of wide pastures, … sleepless, and ever awake;
"To whom Ahura Mazda offered up a sacrifice in the shining Garo-nmana.

124. "With his arms lifted up towards Immortality, Mithra, the lord of wide pastures, drives forward from the shining Garo-nmana, in a beautiful chariot that drives on, ever-swift, adorned with all sorts of ornaments, and made of gold.

125. "Four stallions draw that chariot, all of the same white colour, living on heavenly food and undying. The hoofs of their fore-feet are shod with gold, the hoofs of their hind-feet are shod with silver; all are yoked to the same pole, and wear the yoke and the cross-beams of the yoke, fastened with hooks of Khshathra vairya to a beautiful. . . .

126. "At his right hand drives Rashnu-Razishta, the most beneficent and most well-shapen.
"At his left hand drives the most upright Chista, the holy one, bearing libations in her hands, clothed with white clothes, and white herself; and the cursing thought of the Law of Mazda.

127. "Close by him drives the strong cursing thought of the wise man, opposing foes in the shape of a boar, a sharp-toothed he-boar, a sharp-jawed boar, that kills at one stroke, pursuing, wrathful, with a dripping face, strong and swift to run, and rushing all around.
"Behind him drives Atar, all in a blaze, and the awful kingly Glory.

128. "On a side of the chariot of Mithra, the lord of wide pastures, stand a thousand bows well-made, with a string of cowgut; they go through the heavenly space, they fall through the heavenly space upon the skulls of the Daevas.

129. "On a side of the chariot of Mithra, the lord of wide pastures, stand a thousand vulture-feathered arrows, with a golden mouth, with a horn shaft, with a brass tail, and well-made. They go through the heavenly space, they fall through the heavenly space upon the skulls of the Daevas.

130. "On a side of the chariot of Mithra, the lord of wide pastures, stand a thousand spears well-made and sharp-piercing. They go through the heavenly space, they fall through the heavenly space upon the skulls of the Daevas.
"On a side of the chariot of Mithra, the lord of wide pastures, stand a thousand steel-hammers, two-edged, well-made. They go through the heavenly space, they fall through the heavenly space upon the skulls of the Daevas.

131. "On a side of the chariot of Mithra, the lord of wide pastures, stand a thousand swords, two-edged and well-made. They go through the heavenly space, they fall through the heavenly space upon the skulls of the Daevas.
"On a side of the chariot of Mithra, the lord of wide pastures, stand a thousand maces of iron, well-made. They go through the heavenly space, they fall through the heavenly space upon the skulls of the Daevas.

132. "On a side of the chariot of Mithra, the lord of wide pastures, stands a beautiful well-falling club, with a hundred knots, a hundred edges, that rushes forward and fells men down; a club cast out of red brass, of strong, golden brass; the strongest of all weapons, the most victorious of all weapons. It goes through the heavenly space, it falls through the heavenly space upon the skulls of the Daevas.

133. After he has smitten the Daevas, after he has smitten down the men who lied unto Mithra, Mithra, the lord of wide pastures, drives forward through Arezahe and Savahe, through Fradadhafshu and Vidadhafshu, through Vourubareshti and Vouru-jareshti, through this our Karshvare, the bright Hvaniratha.

134. "Angra Mainyu, who is all death, flees away in fear; Aeshma, the evil-doing Peshotanu, flees away in fear; the long-handed Bushyasta flees away in fear; all the Daevas unseen and the Varenya fiends flee away in fear.

135. "Oh! may we never fall across the rush of Mithra, the lord of wide pastures, when in anger! May Mithra, the lord of wide pastures, never smite us in his anger; he who stands up upon this earth as the strongest of all gods, the most valiant of all gods, the most energetic of all gods, the swiftest of all gods, the most fiend-smiting of all gods, he, Mithra, the lord of wide pastures.

"For his brightness and glory, I will offer him a sacrifice worth being heard. ...

XXXII.

136. "We sacrifice unto Mithra, the lord of wide pastures, ... sleepless, and ever awake;
"For whom white stallions, yoked to his chariot, draw it, on one golden wheel, with a full shining axle.

137. "If Mithra takes his libations to his own dwelling, "Happy that man, I think,"—said Ahura Mazda, "O holy Zarathra! for whom a holy priest, as pious as any in the world, who is the Word incarnate, offers up a sacrifice unto Mithra with bundles of baresma and with the [proper] words.

"'straight to that man, I think, will Mithra come, to visit his dwelling,

138. "'When Mithra's boons will come to him, as he follows God's teaching, and thinks according to God's teaching. ""Woe to that man, I think,"—said Ahura Mazda,—"O holy Zarathushtra! for whom an unholy priest, not pious, who is not the Word incarnate, stands behind the baresma, however full may be the bundles of baresma he ties, however long may be the sacrifice he performs."

139. "He does not delight Ahura Mazda, nor the other Amesha-Spentas, nor Mithra, the lord of wide pastures, he who thus scorns Mazda, and the other Amesha-Spentas, and Mithra, the lord of wide pastures, and the Law, and Rashnu, and Arstat, who makes the world grow, who makes the world increase.

"For his brightness and glory, I will offer him a sacrifice worth being heard. ...

XXXIII.

140. "We sacrifice unto Mithra, the lord of wide pastures, ... sleepless, and ever awake.
"I will offer up a sacrifice unto the good Mithra, O Spitama! unto the strong, heavenly god, who is foremost, highly merciful, and peerless; whose house is above, a stout and strong warrior;

141. "Victorious and armed with a well-fashioned weapon, watchful in darkness and undeceivable. He is the stoutest of the stoutest, he is the strongest of the strongest, he is the most intelligent of the gods, he is victorious and endowed with Glory: he, of the ten thousand eyes, of the ten thousand spies, the powerful, all-knowing, undeceivable god.
"For his brightness and glory, I will offer him a sacrifice worth being heard. ...

XXXIV.

142. "We sacrifice unto Mithra, the lord of wide pastures, ... sleepless, and ever awake;
"Who, with his manifold knowledge, powerfully increases the creation of Spenta Mainyu, and is a well-created and most great Yazata, self-shining like the moon, when he makes his own body shine;

143. "Whose face is flashing with light like the face of the star Tistrya; whose chariot is embraced by that goddess who is foremost amongst those who have no deceit in them, O Spitama! who is fairer than any creature in the world, and full of light to shine. I will worship that chariot, wrought by the Maker, Ahura Mazda, inlaid with stars and made of a heavenly substance; (the chariot) of Mithra, who has ten thousand spies, the powerful, all-knowing, undeceivable god.
"For his brightness and glory, I will offer him a sacrifice worth being heard. ...

XXXV.

144. "We sacrifice unto Mithra, the lord of wide pastures, who is truth-speaking, a chief in assemblies, with a thousand ears, well-shapen, with a thousand eyes, high, with full knowledge, strong, sleepless, and ever awake.
"We sacrifice unto the Mithra around countries; "We sacrifice unto the Mithra within countries; "We sacrifice unto the Mithra in this country; "We sacrifice unto the Mithra above countries; "We sacrifice unto the Mithra under countries; "We sacrifice unto the Mithra before countries; "We sacrifice unto the Mithra behind countries.

145.   "We sacrifice unto Mithra and Ahura, the two great, imperishable, holy gods; and unto the stars, and the moon, and the sun, with the trees that yield up baresma. We sacrifice unto Mithra, the lord of all countries.

"For his brightness and glory, I will offer unto him a sacrifice worth being heard, namely, unto Mithra, the lord of wide pastures.

"Yatha ahu vairyo: The will of the Lord is the law of holiness. ...

"I bless the sacrifice and p yer, and the strength and vigour of Mithra, the lord of wide pastures, who has a thousand ears, ten thousand eyes, a Yazata invoked by his own name; and that of Rama Hvastra.

"Ashem Vohu: Holiness is the best of all good. ...

"[Give] unto that man brightness and glory, ... give him the bright, all-happy, blissful abode of the holy Ones!"

Hymns to Soma
Vedic Sanskrit 1500 BCE

SOMA HYMN

Wisely I have partaken of the sweet food that stirs good thoughts, best banisher of care, to which all gods and mortals, calling it honey, come together.

If thou hast entered within, thou shalt be Aditi, appeaser of divine wrath. Mayest thou, O Indu, enjoying the friendship of Indra, like an obedient mare the pole, advance us to wealth.

We have drunk Soma; we have become immortal; we have gone to the light; we have found the gods. What can hostility now do to use, and what the malice of mortal man, O immortal one?

Do good to our heart when drunk, O Indu; kindly like a father, O Soma, to his son, thoughtful like a friend to his friend, O far-famed one, prolong our years that we may live, O Soma.

These glorious, freedom-giving [drops], ye have knit me together in my joints like straps a car; let those drops protect me from breaking a leg and save me from disease.

Like fire kindled by friction inflame me; illumine us; make us wealthier. For then, in thy intoxication, O Soma, I regard myself as rich. Enter [into us] for prosperity.

Of thee pressed with devoted mind we would partake as of paternal wealth. King Soma, prolong out years as the sun the days of spring.

King Soma, be gracious to us for welfare; we are thy devotees; know that. There arise might and wrath, O Indu: abandon us not according to the desire of our foe.

The Rig Veda, trans. Ralph T. H. Griffith. Copyright in the Public Domain.

Since thou art the protector of our body, O Soma, thou as surveyor of men has settled in every limb. If we infringe thine ordinances, then be gracious to us as our good friend, O god, for higher welfare.

I would associate with the wholesome friend who having been drunk would not injure me,O lord of the bays. For [the enjoyment of] that Some which has been deposited in us, I approach Indra to prolong our years.

Those ailments have started off, diseases have sped away, the powers of darkness have been affrighted. Some has mounted in us with might: we have gone to where men prolong their years.

The drop drunk in our hearts, O Fathers, that immortal has entered us mortals, to that Soma we would pay worship with oblation; we would abide in his mercy and good graces.

Thou, O Soma, uniting with the Fathers, hast extended thyself over Heaven and Earth. To thee as such, O Indu, we would pay worship with oblation: we would be lords of riches.

Ye protecting gods, speak for us. Let not sleep overpower us, nor idle talk. We always dear to Soma, rich in strong sons, would utter divine worship.

Thou art, O Soma, a giver of strength to us on all sides. Thou art a finder of light. Do thou, as surveyor of men, enter us. Do thou, O Indu, protect us behind and before with thine aids accordant.

The Gathas of
Zarathustra
(Zoroaster)
Old Avestan 1000–600 BCE

YASNA 30 (AVESTA)

1) And in this way I will say to those arriving ones those things which should be considered even if known, to praise the Ahura (Lord), worship Vahu Manah (Good Mind), oh those who have good insight are worthy to be seen by the visible joy who he shall see bliss.

2) Hear the best with your ears, reflect with pure thought, with preference each single man's decision for his own body, before the great decision (End of Time) waiting for himself to declare in four of us.

3) At first these two spirits who were twin, they made themselves manifest in a dream, in thought and word and action, the better and the evil they are two, the beneficent distinguished the right, the maleficent did not.

4) Then when these two spirits came together, at first they gave life and non-life so that at last there should be hell belonging for Druj (Lie), but heaven for the Ashavan (Righteous)

5) Of those two spirits the one belonging to Druj chose to do the worst, most Beneficent Spirit (chose) Truth who was clothed in hardest stone who shall satisfy Ahura continuously throughout the work of the wise one.

6) The Daivas (Old/False Gods) did not choose correct between them when conferring, since they chose worst thing, thus they ran together into rage by which may existence.

7) And if to it he comes by power, Good Thought and Truth, then lasting appearance, devotedness will be given the souls so that among (people) one will ... so that he be the first among you during retribution (Day of Final Judgment).

8) And when punishment to these sins shall have come then, oh Mazda (Wise Lord) for ... by Good Thought, certainly help them declare, oh Ahura, who (you) give Druj to the hands of Truth

9) And so we may be who will make the world perfect (renovated), oh Mazda and other Gods, bringer of change by Truth when our thoughts will have come together in order for their thoughts to change

10) For then destruction will descend upon the prosperity of Druj, then the swiftest (horse) will race ahead, oh Mazda and Truth have ...

CYRUS THE GREAT
ROYAL PROCLAMATION

[1–8] When […] of the four quarters. […] An incompetent person [i.e., Nabonidus] was installed to exercise lordship over his country. […] he imposed upon them. An imitation of Esagila he made, and […] for Ur and the rest of the cultic centers, a ritual which was improper to them, an unholy display offering without […] fear he daily recited. Irreverently, he put an end to the regular offerings and he interfered in the cultic centers; […] he established in the sacred centers. By his own plan, he did away with the worship of Marduk, the king of the gods, he continually did evil against Marduk's city. Daily, […] without interruption, he imposed the corvée upon its inhabitants unrelentingly, ruining them all.

[9–11] Upon hearing their cries, the lord of the gods became furiously angry and […] their borders; the gods who lived among them forsook their dwellings, angry that he [sc. Nabonidus] had brought them to Babylon. Marduk, the exalted, the lord of the gods, turned towards all the habitations that were abandoned and all the people of Sumer and Akkad, who had become corpses. He was reconciled and had mercy upon them.

[11–14] Marduk surveyed and looked throughout the lands, searching for a righteous king, his favorite. He called out his name: Cyrus, king of Anšan; he pronounced his name to be king all over the world. He made the land of Gutium and all the Umman-manda [i.e., the Medes] bow in submission at his feet. And he [i.e., Cyrus] shepherded with justice and righteousness all the black-headed people, over whom he [i.e., Marduk] had given him victory. Marduk, the great lord, guardian of his people, looked with gladness upon his good deeds and upright heart.

[15–19] He ordered him to go to his city Babylon. He set him on the road to Babylon and like a companion and a friend, he went at his side. His vast army, whose number, like water of the river, cannot be known, marched at his side fully armed. He made him enter his city Babylon without fighting or battle; he saved Babylon from hardship. He delivered Nabonidus, the king who did not revere him, into his hands. All the people of Babylon, all the land of Sumer and Akkad, princes and governors, bowed to him and kissed his feet. They rejoiced at his kingship and their faces shone. Lord by whose aid the dead were revived and who had all been redeemed from hardship and difficulty, they greeted him with gladness and praised his name.

[20–22a] I am Cyrus, king of the world, great king, mighty king, king of Babylon, king of Sumer and Akkad, king of the four quarters, the son of Cambyses, great king, king of Anšan, grandson of Cyrus, great king, king of Anšan, descendant of Teispes, great king, king of Anšan, of an eternal line of kingship, whose rule Bêl and Nabu love, whose kingship they desire for their hearts' pleasure.

[22b-28] When I entered Babylon in a peaceful manner, I took up my lordly abode in the royal palace amidst rejoicing and happiness. Marduk, the great lord, established as his fate for me a magnanimous heart of one who loves Babylon, and I daily attended to his worship. My vast army marched into Babylon in peace; I did not permit anyone to frighten the people of Sumer and Akkad. I sought the welfare of the city of Babylon and all its sacred centers. As for the citizens of Babylon, […] upon whom Nabonidus imposed a corvée which was not the gods' wish and not befitting them, I relieved their wariness and freed them from their service. Marduk, the great lord, rejoiced over my good deeds. He sent gracious blessing upon me, Cyrus, the king who worships him, and upon Cambyses, the son who is my offspring, and upon all my army, and in peace, before him, we moved around in friendship.

[28–33] By his exalted word, all the kings who sit upon thrones throughout the world, from the Upper Sea to the Lower Sea [*i.e., from the Mediterranean Sea to the Persian Gulf*], who live in the districts far-off, the kings of the West, who dwell in tents, all of them, brought their heavy tribute before me and in Babylon they kissed my feet. From Babylon to Aššur and from Susa, Agade, Ešnunna, Zamban, Me-Turnu, Der, as far as the region of Gutium, the sacred centers on the other side of the Tigris, whose sanctuaries had been abandoned for a long time, I returned the images of the gods, who had resided there [i.e., in Babylon], to their places and I let them dwell in eternal abodes. I gathered all their inhabitants and returned to them their dwellings. In addition, at the command of Marduk, the great lord, I settled in their habitations, in pleasing abodes, the gods of Sumer and Akkad, whom Nabonidus, to the anger of the lord of the gods, had brought into Babylon.

[34–36] May all the gods whom I settled in their sacred centers ask daily of Bêl and Nâbu that my days be long and may they intercede for my welfare. May they say to Marduk, my lord: "As for Cyrus, the king who reveres you, and Cambyses, his son, [*lacuna*]." The people of Babylon blessed my kingship, and I settled all the lands in peaceful abodes.

[37–44] I daily increased the number offerings to […] geese, two ducks, and ten turledoves above the former offerings of geese, ducks, and turtledoves. […] Dur-Imgur-Enlil, the great wall of Babylon, its de[fen]se, I sought to strengthen […] The quay wall of brick, which a former king had bu[ilt, but had not com]pleted its construction, […] who had not surrounded the city on the outside, which no former king had made, who a levy of workmen had led into of Babylon, […] with bitumen and bricks, I built anew and completed their job. […] magnificent gates I overlaid in copper, treshholds and pivots of cast bronze I fixed in their doorways. […] An inscription with the name of Aššurbanipal, a king who had preceded me, I saw in its midst. […] for eternity.

Isaiah 44–45

²⁴ "This is what the LORD says—
your Redeemer, who formed you in the womb:
I am the LORD,
who has made all things,
who alone stretched out the heavens,
who spread out the earth by myself,
²⁵ who foils the signs of false prophets
and makes fools of diviners,
who overthrows the learning of the wise
and turns it into nonsense,
²⁶ who carries out the words of his servants
and fulfills the predictions of his messengers, who says of Jerusalem, "It shall
be inhabited," of the towns of Judah, "They shall be built," and of their ruins,
"I will restore them,"
²⁷ who says to the watery deep, "Be dry,
and I will dry up your streams,"
²⁸ who says of Cyrus, "He is my shepherd
and will accomplish all that I please;
he will say of Jerusalem, "Let it be rebuilt,"
and of the temple, "Let its foundations be laid.""

ISAIAH 45

¹ "This is what the LORD says to his anointed, to Cyrus, whose right hand I take hold of to subdue nations before him and to strip kings of their armor, to open doors before him so that gates will not be shut:

² I will go before you
and will level the mountains; I will break down gates of bronze and cut through bars of iron.

³ I will give you the treasures of darkness, riches stored in secret places,
so that you may know that I am the LORD, the God of Israel, who summons you by name.

⁴ For the sake of Jacob my servant, of Israel my chosen, I summon you by name and bestow on you a title of honor, though you do not acknowledge me.

⁵ I am the LORD, and there is no other; apart from me there is no God. I will strengthen you, though you have not acknowledged me,

⁶ so that from the rising of the sun
to the place of its setting
men may know there is none besides me.
I am the LORD, and there is no other.

⁷ I form the light and create darkness,
I bring prosperity and create disaster; I, the LORD, do all these things.

⁸ "You heavens above, rain down righteousness;
let the clouds shower it down. Let the earth open wide, let salvation spring up, let righteousness grow with it; I, the LORD, have created it.

⁹ "Woe to him who quarrels with his Maker,
to him who is but a potsherd among the potsherds on the ground. Does the clay say to the potter, "What are you making?" Does your work say, "He has no hands"?

¹⁰ Woe to him who says to his father,
"What have you begotten?"
or to his mother,
"What have you brought to birth?"

¹¹ "This is what the LORD says—
the Holy One of Israel, and its Maker: Concerning things to come,
do you question me about my children,
or give me orders about the work of my hands?

¹² It is I who made the earth and created mankind upon it. My own hands stretched out the heavens; I marshaled their starry hosts.

¹³ I will raise up Cyrus in my righteousness: I will make all his ways straight. He will rebuild my city and set my exiles free, but not for a price or reward, says the LORD Almighty."

¹⁴ This is what the LORD says:

"The products of Egypt and the merchandise of Cush,
and those tall Sabeans—
they will come over to you
and will be yours;
they will trudge behind you,
coming over to you in chains.
They will bow down before you
and plead with you, saying,
"Surely God is with you, and there is no other;
there is no other god."

¹⁵ Truly you are a God who hides himself,
O God and Savior of Israel.

¹⁶ All the makers of idols will be put to shame and disgraced;
they will go off into disgrace together.

¹⁷ But Israel will be saved by the LORD
with an everlasting salvation;
you will never be put to shame or disgraced,
to ages everlasting.

¹⁸ For this is what the LORD says—
he who created the heavens,
he is God;
he who fashioned and made the earth,
he founded it;
he did not create it to be empty,
but formed it to be inhabited—
he says:
"I am the LORD,
and there is no other.

¹⁹ I have not spoken in secret,
from somewhere in a land of darkness;
I have not said to Jacob's descendants,
"Seek me in vain."
I, the LORD, speak the truth;
I declare what is right.

²⁰ "Gather together and come;

assemble, you fugitives from the nations. Ignorant are those who carry about idols of wood, who pray to gods that cannot save.

²¹ Declare what is to be, present it—
let them take counsel together.
Who foretold this long ago,
who declared it from the distant past?
Was it not I, the LORD?
And there is no God apart from me,
a righteous God and a Savior;
there is none but me.

²² "Turn to me and be saved,
all you ends of the earth;
for I am God, and there is no other.

²³ By myself I have sworn,
my mouth has uttered in all integrity a word that will not be revoked: Before me every knee will bow; by me every tongue will swear.

²⁴ They will say of me, "In the LORD alone
are righteousness and strength."
All who have raged against him
will come to him and be put to shame.

²⁵ But in the LORD all the descendants of Israel
will be found righteous and will exult.

DARIUS I:
BEHISTUN
INSCRIPTION
ACHAMENID OLD PERSIAN

I am Darius, great king, king of kings, king of countries, an Achaemenid, king of all men, a Persian, the king of Persia, Darius the king says: My father is Hystaspes, the father of Hystaspes is Arsamnes, the father of Arsamnes is Ariaramnes, the father of Ariaramnes is Tispish, the father of Tispish is Achaemenes … Darius the king says: By the will of Ahuramazda I am king. Ahuramazda redelivered the kingship to me, Darius the king says: these are the countries which came to me. By the will of Ahuramazda they became my subjects, they bore me tribute. Day and night they did what I told them. Darius the king says: Among these countries, whatever man was loyal I treated well, but whom ever was unruly I punished well. By the will of Ahuramazda these countries behaved according to my law. They did as I told them. Darius the king says: Ahuramazda delivered this kingship to me. Ahuramazda bore me aid until I had secured this empire. By the will of Ahuramazda I hold this empire.

Darius the kings says: This is what I did by the will of Ahuramazda in the same year after I became king. I fought 19 battles. By the will of Ahuramazda I won them. And I captured 9 kings. One named Gaumata was a Magi. He lied, thus he said, "I am Bardiys, the son of Cyrus." He made Persis rebellious. Darius the king says: I captured these 9 kings in these battles. Darius the king says: these are the countries which became rebellious. The Lie made them rebellious, because these kings lied to the people. Afterward Ahuramazda placed them in my hands. I dealt with them at my pleasure. Darius the king says: You, whoever you are who shall be king afterward, guard yourself diligently from the Lie. Punish well that man who shall be a liar, if you should think, "My country shall be secure." You, whoever you are who shall afterward read this inscription which I made, may it convince you. Do not think that this is a lie. Darius the king says: O Ahuramazda, I swear this oath, that this is true; it is not a lie; I did this in one and the same year.

Now let this convince you. Thus tell the people what I have done; do not conceal it. If you do not conceal this proclamation and tell it to the people, may Ahuramazda be a friend to you and may your family be numerous and may you live long. Darius the king says: If you should conceal this proclamation and not tell it to the people, may Ahuramazda smite you and may you have not family. Darius the king says: this is what 1 did; in one and the same year I did it by the will of Ahuramazda. Ahuramazda bore me aid, as did also the other gods who exist. Ahuramazda bore me aid, as did also the other gods who exist, for the reason that I was not unruly, I was not a liar, I was not an evildoer, neither I nor my family transgressed. I did not deal crookedly with either the weak or the strong. I treated him well who cooperated with my house; I punished him well who sought to destroy it.

STORY OF YIMA
AVESTA (VENDIDAD)

1. Zarathushtra (Prophet) asked Ahura Mazda (Supreme God):
    O Ahura Mazda, most beneficent Spirit, Maker of the material world, thou Holy One!
    Who was the first mortal, before myself, Zarathushtra, with whom thou, Ahura Mazda, didst converse[1], whom thou didst teach the Religion of Ahura, the Religion of Zarathushtra?
2. Ahura Mazda answered: The fair Yima, the good shepherd, O holy Zarathushtra! he was the first mortal, before thee, Zarathushtra, with whom I, Ahura Mazda, did converse, whom I taught the Religion of Ahura, the Religion of Zarathushtra.
3. Unto him, O Zarathushtra, I, Ahura Mazda, spoke, saying: "Well, fair Yima, son of Vivanghat, be thou the preacher and the bearer of my Religion!" And the fair Yima, O Zarathushtra, replied unto me, saying: "I was not born, I was not taught to be the preacher and the bearer of thy Religion."
4. Then I, Ahura Mazda, said thus unto him, O Zarathushtra: "Since thou dost not consent to be the preacher and the bearer of my Religion, then make thou my world increase, make my world grow: consent thou to nourish, to rule, and to watch over my world."
5. And the fair Yima replied unto me, O Zarathushtra, saying: "Yes! I will make thy world increase, I will make thy world grow. Yes! I will nourish, and rule, and watch over thy world. There shall be, while I am king, neither cold wind not hot wind, neither disease nor death."

6. Then I, Ahura Mazda, brought two implements unto him: a golden seal and a poniard inlaid with gold. Behold, here Yima bears the royal sway!

7. [Obscure.]

8. Thus, under the sway of Yima, three hundred winters passed away, and the earth was replenished with flocks and herds, with men and dogs and birds and with red blazing fires, and there was room no more for flocks, herds, and men.

9. Then I warned the fair Yima, saying: "O fair Yima, son of Vivanghat, the earth has become full of flocks and herds, of men and dogs and birds and of red blazing fires, and there is room no more for flocks, herds, and men."

10. Then Yima stepped forward, in light, southwards, on the way of the sun, and (afterwards) he pressed the earth with the golden seal, and bored it with the poniard, speaking thus: (Holy Angle) "O Spenta Armaiti, kindly open asunder and stretch thyself afar, to bear flocks and herds and men."

11. And Yima made the earth grow larger by one-third than it was before, and there came flocks and herds and men, at their will and wish, as many as he wished.

12. Thus, under the sway of Yima, six hundred winters passed away, and the earth was replenished with flocks and herds, with men and dogs and birds and with red blazing fires, and there was room no more for flocks, herds, and men.

13. And I warned the fair Yima, saying: "O fair Yima, son of Vivanghat, the earth has become full of flocks and herds, of men and dogs and birds and of red blazing fires, and there is room no more for flocks, herds, and men."

14. Then Yima stepped forward, in light, southwards, on the way of the sun, and (afterwards) he pressed the earth with the golden seal, and bored it with the poniard, speaking thus: (Holy Angle) "O Spenta Armaiti, kindly) open asunder and stretch thyself afar, to bear flocks and herds and men."

15. And Yima made the earth grow larger by two-thirds than it was before, and there came flocks and herds and men, at their will and wish, as many as he wished.

16. Thus, under the sway of Yima, nine hundred winters passed away, and the earth was replenished with flocks and herds, with men and dogs and birds and with red blazing fires, and there was room no more for flocks, herds, and men.

17. And I warned the fair Yima, saying: "O fair Yima, son of Vivanghat, the earth has become full of flocks and herds, of men and dogs and birds and of red blazing fires, and there is room no more for flocks, herds, and men."

18. Then Yima stepped forward, in light, southwards, on the way of the sun, and (afterwards) he pressed the earth with the golden seal, and bored it with the poniard, speaking thus: (Holy Angle) "O Spenta Armaiti, kindly open asunder and stretch thyself afar, to bear flocks and herds and men."

19. And Yima made the earth grow larger by two-thirds than it was before, and there came flocks and herds and men, at their will and wish, as many as he wished.

II.

20. The Maker, Ahura Mazda, called together a meeting of the celestial Yazatas in the (Aryan Homeland) Airyana Vaejo of high renown, by the (River) Vanguhi Daitya. The fair Yima, the good shepherd, called together a meeting of the best of the mortals[12], in the Airyana Vaejo of high renown, by the Vanguhi Daitya.

21. To that meeting came Ahura Mazda, in the Airyana Vaejo of high renown, by the Vanguhi Daitya; he came together with the celestial Yazatas. To that meeting came the fair Yima, the good shepherd, in the Airyana Vaejo of high renown, by the Vanguhi Daitya; he came together with the best of the mortals.

22. And Ahura Mazda spoke unto Yima, saying: "O fair Yima, son of Vivanghat! Upon the material world the evil winters are about to fall, that shall bring the fierce, deadly frost; upon the material world the evil winters are about to fall, that shall make snowflakes fall thick, even an aredvi deep on the highest tops of mountains.

23. "And the beasts that live in the wilderness[15], and those that live on the tops of the mountains[16], and those that live in the bosom of the dale[17] shall take shelter in underground abodes.

24. "Before that winter, the country would bear plenty of grass for cattle, before the waters had flooded it. Now after the melting of the snow, O Yima, a place wherein the footprint of a sheep may be seen will be a wonder in the world.

25. "Therefore make thee a (enclosure) Vara, long as a riding-ground on every side of the square, and thither bring the seeds of sheep and oxen, of men, of dogs, of birds, and of red blazing fires. Therefore make thee a Vara, long as a riding-ground on every side of the square, to be an abode for man; a Vara, long as a riding-ground on every side of the square, for oxen and sheep.

26. "There thou shalt make waters flow in a bed a hathra long; there thou shalt settle birds, on the green that never fades, with food that never fails. There thou shalt establish dwelling-places, consisting of a house with a balcony, a courtyard, and as gallery.

27. "Thither thou shalt bring the seeds of men and women, of the greatest, best, and finest on this earth[21]; thither thou shalt bring the seeds of every kind of cattle, of the greatest, best, and finest on this earth.

28. "Thither thou shalt bring the seeds of every kind of tree, of the highest of size and sweetest of odor on this earth[22]; thither thou shalt bring the seeds of every kind of fruit, the best of savour and sweetest of odour[23]. All those seeds shalt thou bring, two of every kind, to be kept inexhaustible there, so long as those men shall stay in the Vara.

29. "There shall be no humpbacked, none bulged forward there; no impotent, no lunatic; no malicious, no liar; no one spiteful, none jealous; no one with decayed tooth,

no leprous to be pent up, nor any of the brands wherewith Angra Mainyu stamps the bodies of mortals.

30. "In the largest part of the place thou shalt make nine streets, six in the middle part, three in the smallest. To the streets of the largest part thou shalt bring a thousand seeds of men and women; to the streets of the middle part, six hundred; to the streets of the smallest part, three hundred[26]. That Vara thou shalt seal up with thy golden seal, and thou shalt make a door, and a window self-shining within.

31. Then Yima said within himself: "How shall I manage to make that Vara which Ahura Mazda has commanded me to make?" And Ahura Mazda said unto Yima: "O fair Yima, son of Vivanghat! Crush the earth with a stamp of thy heel, and then knead it with thy hands, as the potter does when kneading the potter's clay.

32. [And Yima did as Ahura Mazda wished; he crushed the earth with a stamp of his heel, he kneaded it with his hands, as the potter does when kneading the potter's clay.]

33. And Yima made a (enclosure) Vara, long as a riding-ground on every side of the square. There he brought the seeds of sheep and oxen, of men, of dogs, of birds, and of red blazing fires. He made a Vara, long as a riding-ground on every side of the square, to be an abode for men; a Vara, long as a riding-ground on every side of the square, for oxen and sheep.

34. There he made waters flow in a bed a hathra long; there he settled birds, on the green that never fades, with food that never fails. There he established dwelling-places, consisting of a house with a balcony, a courtyard, and a gallery.

35. There he brought the seeds of men and women, of the greatest, best, and finest on this earth; there he brought the seeds of every kind of cattle, of the greatest, best, and finest on this earth.

36. There he brought the seeds of every kind of tree, of the highest of size and sweetest of odor on this earth; there he brought the seeds of every kind of fruit, the best of savour and sweetest of odor. All those seeds he brought, two of every kind, to be kept inexhaustible there, so long as those men shall stay in the (enclosure) Vara.

37. And there were no humpbacked, none bulged forward there; no impotent, no lunatic; no one malicious, no liar; no one spiteful, none jealous; no one with decayed tooth, no leprous to be pent up, nor any of the brands wherewith (Evil Spirit) Angra Mainyu stamps the bodies of mortals.

38. In the largest part of the place he made nine streets, six in the middle part, three in the smallest. To the streets of the largest part he brought a thousand seeds of men and women; to the streets of the middle part, six hundred; to the streets of the smallest part, three hundred. That Vara he sealed up with the golden ring, and he made a door, and a window self-shining within.

39. O Maker of the material world, thou Holy One! What are the lights that give light in the Vara which Yima made?

40. Ahura Mazda answered: "There are uncreated lights and created lights. The one thing missed there is the sight of the stars, the moon, and the sun, and a year seems only as a day.

41. "Every fortieth year, to every couple two are born, a male and a female. And thus it is for every sort of cattle. And the men in the Vara which Yima made live the happiest life

42. O Maker of the material world, thou Holy One! Who is he who brought the Religion of Mazda into the Vara which Yima made? Ahura Mazda answered: "It was the bird Karshipta, O holy Zarathushtra!"

43. O Maker of the material world, thou Holy One! Who are the Lord and the Master there? Ahura Mazda answered: "Urvatat-nara[35], O Zarathushtra! and thyself, Zarathushtra."

THE
BHAGAVADGITA
MAHABHARATA
(5TH–2ND BCE)

SANSKRIT

Dialogue between Lord Krishna and Arjuna before the great battle (Chapter 2):

Sañjaya said: Seeing Arjuna full of compassion, his mind depressed, his eyes full of tears, Madhusūdana, Krsna, spoke the following words.

The Supreme Personality of Godhead said: My dear Arjuna, how have these impurities come upon you? They are not at all befitting a man who knows the value of life. They lead not to higher planets but to infamy.

O son of Prthā, do not yield to this degrading impotence. It does not become you. Give up such petty weakness of heart and arise, O chastiser of the enemy.

Arjuna said: O killer of enemies, O killer of Madhu, how can I counterattack with arrows in battle men like Bhīsma and Drona, who are worthy of my worship?

It would be better to live in this world by begging than to live at the cost of the lives of great souls who are my teachers. Even though desiring worldly gain, they are superiors. If they are killed, everything we enjoy will be tainted with blood.

Nor do we know which is better—conquering them or being conquered by them. If we killed the sons of Dhrtarāstra, we should not care to live. Yet they are now standing before us on the battlefield.

The Mahabharata of Krishna-Dwaipayana Vyasa, trans. Kisari Mohan Ganguli. Copyright in the Public Domain.

Now I am confused about my duty and have lost all composure because of miserly weakness. In this condition I am asking You to tell me for certain what is best for me. Now I am Your disciple, and a soul surrendered unto You. Please instruct me.

I can find no means to drive away this grief which is drying up my senses. I will not be able to dispel it even if I win a prosperous, unrivaled kingdom on earth with sovereignty like the demigods in heaven.

Sañjaya said: Having spoken thus, Arjuna, chastiser of enemies, told Kṛṣṇa, "Govinda, I shall not fight," and fell silent.

O descendant of Bharata, at that time Kṛṣṇa, smiling, in the midst of both the armies, spoke the following words to the grief-stricken Arjuna.

The Supreme Personality of Godhead said: While speaking learned words, you are mourning for what is not worthy of grief. Those who are wise lament neither for the living nor for the dead.

Never was there a time when I did not exist, nor you, nor all these kings; nor in the future shall any of us cease to be.

As the embodied soul continuously passes, in this body, from boyhood to youth to old age, the soul similarly passes into another body at death. A sober person is not bewildered by such a change.

O son of Kuntī, the nonpermanent appearance of happiness and distress, and their disappearance in due course, are like the appearance and disappearance of winter and summer seasons. They arise from sense perception, O scion of Bharata, and one must learn to tolerate them without being disturbed.

O best among men [Arjuna], the person who is not disturbed by happiness and distress and is steady in both is certainly eligible for liberation.

Those who are seers of the truth have concluded that of the nonexistent [the material body] there is no endurance and of the eternal [the soul] there is no change. This they have concluded by studying the nature of both.

That which pervades the entire body you should know to be indestructible. No one is able to destroy that imperishable soul.

The material body of the indestructible, immeasurable and eternal living entity is sure to come to an end; therefore, fight, O descendant of Bharata.

Neither he who thinks the living entity the slayer nor he who thinks it slain is in knowledge, for the self slays not nor is slain.

For the soul there is neither birth nor death at any time. He has not come into being, does not come into being, and will not come into being. He is unborn, eternal, ever-existing and primeval. He is not slain when the body is slain.

O Pārtha, how can a person who knows that the soul is indestructible, eternal, unborn and immutable kill anyone or cause anyone to kill?

As a person puts on new garments, giving up old ones, the soul similarly accepts new material bodies, giving up the old and useless ones.

The soul can never be cut to pieces by any weapon, nor burned by fire, nor moistened by water, nor withered by the wind.

This individual soul is unbreakable and insoluble, and can be neither burned nor dried. He is everlasting, present everywhere, unchangeable, immovable and eternally the same.

It is said that the soul is invisible, inconceivable and immutable. Knowing this, you should not grieve for the body.

If, however, you think that the soul [or the symptoms of life] is always born and dies forever, you still have no reason to lament, O mighty-armed.

One who has taken his birth is sure to die, and after death one is sure to take birth again. Therefore, in the unavoidable discharge of your duty, you should not lament.

All created beings are un-manifest in their beginning, manifest in their interim state, and un-manifest again when annihilated. So what need is there for lamentation?

Some look on the soul as amazing, some describe him as amazing, and some hear of him as amazing, while others, even after hearing about him, cannot understand him at all.

O descendant of Bharata, he who dwells in the body can never be slain. Therefore you need not grieve for any living being.

Considering your specific duty as a ksatriya, you should know that there is no better engagement for you than fighting on religious principles; and so there is no need for hesitation.

O Pārtha, happy are the ksatriyas to whom such fighting opportunities come unsought, opening for them the doors of the heavenly planets.

If, however, you do not perform your religious duty of fighting, then you will certainly incur sins for neglecting your duties and thus lose your reputation as a fighter.

People will always speak of your infamy, and for a respectable person, dishonor is worse than death.

The great generals who have highly esteemed your name and fame will think that you have left the battlefield out of fear only, and thus they will consider you insignificant.

Your enemies will describe you in many unkind words and scorn your ability. What could be more painful for you?

O son of Kuntī, either you will be killed on the battlefield and attain the heavenly planets, or you will conquer and enjoy the earthly kingdom. Therefore, get up with determination and fight.

Do thou fight for the sake of fighting, without considering happiness or distress, loss or gain, victory or defeat—and by so doing you shall never incur sin.

Thus far I have described this knowledge to you through analytical study. Now listen as I explain it in terms of working without fruitive results. O son of Prthā, when you act in such knowledge you can free yourself from the bondage of works.

In this endeavor there is no loss or diminution, and a little advancement on this path can protect one from the most dangerous type of fear.

Those who are on this path are resolute in purpose, and their aim is one. O beloved child of the Kurus, the intelligence of those who are irresolute is many-branched.

Men of small knowledge are very much attached to the flowery words of the Vedas, which recommend various fruitive activities for elevation to heavenly planets, resultant good birth, power, and so forth. Being desirous of sense gratification and opulent life, they say that there is nothing more than this.

In the minds of those who are too attached to sense enjoyment and material opulence, and who are bewildered by such things, the resolute determination for devotional service to the Supreme Lord does not take place.

The Vedas deal mainly with the subject of the three modes of material nature. O Arjuna, become transcendental to these three modes. Be free from all dualities and from all anxieties for gain and safety, and be established in the self.

All purposes served by a small well can at once be served by a great reservoir of water. Similarly, all the purposes of the Vedas can be served to one who knows the purpose behind them.

You have a right to perform your prescribed duty, but you are not entitled to the fruits of action. Never consider yourself the cause of the results of your activities, and never be attached to not doing your duty.

Perform your duty equipoised, O Arjuna, abandoning all attachment to success or failure. Such equanimity is called yoga.

O Dhanañjaya, keep all abominable activities far distant by devotional service, and in that consciousness surrender unto the Lord. Those who want to enjoy the fruits of their work are misers.

A man engaged in devotional service rids himself of both good and bad actions even in this life. Therefore strive for yoga, which is the art of all work.

By thus engaging in devotional service to the Lord, great sages or devotees free themselves from the results of work in the material world. In this way they become free from the cycle of birth and death and attain the state beyond all miseries [by going back to Godhead].

When your intelligence has passed out of the dense forest of delusion, you shall become indifferent to all that has been heard and all that is to be heard.

When your mind is no longer disturbed by the flowery language of the Vedas, and when it remains fixed in the trance of self-realization, then you will have attained the divine consciousness.

Arjuna said: O Krsna, what are the symptoms of one whose consciousness is thus merged in transcendence? How does he speak, and what is his language? How does he sit, and how does he walk?

The Supreme Personality of Godhead said: O Pārtha, when a man gives up all varieties of desire for sense gratification, which arise from mental concoction, and when his mind, thus purified, finds satisfaction in the self alone, then he is said to be in pure transcendental consciousness.

One who is not disturbed in mind even amidst the threefold miseries or elated when there is happiness, and who is free from attachment, fear and anger, is called a sage of steady mind.

In the material world, one who is unaffected by whatever good or evil he may obtain, neither praising it nor despising it, is firmly fixed in perfect knowledge.

One who is able to withdraw his senses from sense objects, as the tortoise draws its limbs within the shell, is firmly fixed in perfect consciousness.

The embodied soul may be restricted from sense enjoyment, though the taste for sense objects remains. But, ceasing such engagements by experiencing a higher taste, he is fixed in consciousness.

The senses are so strong and impetuous, O Arjuna, that they forcibly carry away the mind even of a man of discrimination who is endeavoring to control them.

One who restrains his senses, keeping them under full control, and fixes his consciousness upon Me, is known as a man of steady intelligence.

While contemplating the objects of the senses, a person develops attachment for them, and from such attachment lust develops, and from lust anger arises.

From anger, complete delusion arises, and from delusion bewilderment of memory. When memory is bewildered, intelligence is lost, and when intelligence is lost one falls down again into the material pool.

But a person free from all attachment and aversion and able to control his senses through regulative principles of freedom can obtain the complete mercy of the Lord.

For one thus satisfied [in Krsna consciousness], the threefold miseries of material existence exist no longer; in such satisfied consciousness, one's intelligence is soon well established.

One who is not connected with the Supreme [in Krsna consciousness] can have neither transcendental intelligence nor a steady mind, without which there is no possibility of peace. And how can there be any happiness without peace?

As a strong wind sweeps away a boat on the water, even one of the roaming senses on which the mind focuses can carry away a man's intelligence.

Therefore, O mighty-armed, one whose senses are restrained from their objects is certainly of steady intelligence.

What is night for all beings is the time of awakening for the self-controlled; and the time of awakening for all beings is night for the introspective sage.

A person who is not disturbed by the incessant flow of desires—that enter like rivers into the ocean, which is ever being filled but is always still—can alone achieve peace, and not the man who strives to satisfy such desires.

A person who has given up all desires for sense gratification, who lives free from desires, who has given up all sense of proprietorship and is devoid of false ego—he alone can attain real peace.

That is the way of the spiritual and godly life, after attaining which a man is not bewildered. If one is thus situated even at the hour of death, one can enter into the kingdom of God.

King Ashoka's Edict After the Battle of Kalinga
Gandhari (Indic)
3rd Century BCE

1. Beloved-of-the-Gods, King Piyadasi, has caused this Dhamma edict to be written. [1] Here (in my domain) no living beings are to be slaughtered or offered in sacrifice. Nor should festivals be held, for Beloved-of-the-Gods, King Piyadasi, sees much to object to in such festivals, although there are some festivals that Beloved-of-the-Gods, King Piyadasi, does approve of.

   Formerly, in the kitchen of Beloved-of-the-Gods, King Piyadasi, hundreds of thousands of animals were killed every day to make curry. But now with the writing of this Dhamma edict only three creatures, two peacocks and a deer are killed, and the deer not always. And in time, not even these three creatures will be killed.

2. Everywhere [2] within Beloved-of-the-Gods, King Piyadasi's domain, and among the people beyond the borders, the Cholas, the Pandyas, the Satiyaputras, the Keralaputras, as far as Tamraparni and where the Greek king Antiochos rules, and among the kings who are neighbors of Antiochos,[3] everywhere has Beloved-of-the-Gods, King Piyadasi, made provision for two types of medical treatment: medical treatment for humans and medical treatment for animals. Wherever medical herbs suitable for humans or animals are not available, I have had them imported and grown. Wherever medical roots or fruits are not available I have had them imported and grown. Along roads I have had wells dug and trees planted for the benefit of humans and animals.[4]

The Edicts of King Asoka: An English Rendering, trans. Ven. S. Dhammika. Copyright © 1993 by Buddhist Publication Society. Reprinted with permission.

3. Beloved-of-the-Gods, King Piyadasi, speaks thus:[5] Twelve years after my corona-
    tion this has been ordered—Everywhere in my domain the Yuktas, the Rajjukas
    and the Pradesikas shall go on inspection tours every five years for the purpose of
    Dhamma instruction and also to conduct other business.[6] Respect for mother and
    father is good, generosity to friends, acquaintances, relatives, Brahmans and ascetics
    is good, not killing living beings is good, moderation in spending and moderation
    in saving is good. The Council shall notify the Yuktas about the observance of these
    instructions in these very words.

4. In the past, for many hundreds of years, killing or harming living beings and im-
    proper behavior towards relatives, and improper behavior towards Brahmans and
    ascetics has increased.[7] But now due to Beloved-of-the-Gods, King Piyadasi's
    Dhamma practice, the sound of the drum has been replaced by the sound of the
    Dhamma.[8] The sighting of heavenly cars, auspicious elephants, bodies of fire
    and other divine sightings has not happened for many hundreds of years. But now
    because Beloved-of-the-Gods, King Piyadasi promotes restraint in the killing and
    harming of living beings, proper behavior towards relatives, Brahmans and ascetics,
    and respect for mother, father and elders, such sightings have increased.[9]
    These and many other kinds of Dhamma practice have been encouraged by
    Beloved-of-the-Gods, King Piyadasi, and he will continue to promote Dhamma
    practice. And the sons, grandsons and great-grandsons of Beloved-of-the-Gods,
    King Piyadasi, too will continue to promote Dhamma practice until the end
    of time; living by Dhamma and virtue, they will instruct in Dhamma. Truly,
    this is the highest work, to instruct in Dhamma. But practicing the Dhamma
    cannot be done by one who is devoid of virtue and therefore its promotion and
    growth is commendable.
    This edict has been written so that it may please my successors to devote them-
    selves to promoting these things and not allow them to decline. Beloved-of-
    the-Gods, King Piyadasi, has had this written twelve years after his coronation.

5. Beloved-of-the-Gods, King Piyadasi, speaks thus:[10] To do good is difficult. One
    who does good first does something hard to do. I have done many good deeds, and,
    if my sons, grandsons and their descendants up to the end of the world act in like
    manner, they too will do much good. But whoever amongst them neglects this, they
    will do evil. Truly, it is easy to do evil.[11]
    In the past there were no Dhamma Mahamatras but such officers were ap-
    pointed by me thirteen years after my coronation. Now they work among all
    religions for the establishment of Dhamma, for the promotion of Dhamma,
    and for the welfare and happiness of all who are devoted to Dhamma. They
    work among the Greeks, the Kambojas, the Gandharas, the Rastrikas, the
    Pitinikas and other peoples on the western borders.[12] They work among
    soldiers, chiefs, Brahmans, householders, the poor, the aged and those devoted

to Dhamma—for their welfare and happiness—so that they may be free from harassment. They (Dhamma Mahamatras) work for the proper treatment of prisoners, towards their unfettering, and if the Mahamatras think, "This one has a family to support," "That one has been bewitched," "This one is old," then they work for the release of such prisoners. They work here, in outlying towns, in the women's quarters belonging to my brothers and sisters, and among my other relatives. They are occupied everywhere. These Dhamma Mahamatras are occupied in my domain among people devoted to Dhamma to determine who is devoted to Dhamma, who is established in Dhamma, and who is generous.

This Dhamma edict has been written on stone so that it might endure long and that my descendants might act in conformity with it.

6. Beloved-of-the-Gods, King Piyadasi, speaks thus: [13] In the past, state business was not transacted nor were reports delivered to the king at all hours. But now I have given this order, that at any time, whether I am eating, in the women's quarters, the bed chamber, the chariot, the palanquin, in the park or wherever, reporters are to be posted with instructions to report to me the affairs of the people so that I might attend to these affairs wherever I am. And whatever I orally order in connection with donations or proclamations, or when urgent business presses itself on the Mahamatras, if disagreement or debate arises in the Council, then it must be reported to me immediately. This is what I have ordered. I am never content with exerting myself or with despatching business. Truly, I consider the welfare of all to be my duty, and the root of this is exertion and the prompt despatch of business. There is no better work than promoting the welfare of all the people and whatever efforts I am making is to repay the debt I owe to all beings to assure their happiness in this life, and attain heaven in the next.

Therefore this Dhamma edict has been written to last long and that my sons, grandsons and great-grandsons might act in conformity with it for the welfare of the world. However, this is difficult to do without great exertion.

7. Beloved-of-the-Gods, King Piyadasi, desires that all religions should reside everywhere, for all of them desire self-control and purity of heart.[14] But people have various desires and various passions, and they may practice all of what they should or only a part of it. But one who receives great gifts yet is lacking in self-control, purity of heart, gratitude and firm devotion, such a person is mean.

8. In the past kings used to go out on pleasure tours during which there was hunting and other entertainment.[15] But ten years after Beloved-of-the-Gods had been coronated, he went on a tour to Sambodhi and thus instituted Dhamma tours.[16] During these tours, the following things took place: visits and gifts to Brahmans and ascetics, visits and gifts of gold to the aged, visits to people in the countryside, instructing them in Dhamma, and discussing Dhamma with them as is suitable. It

is this that delights Beloved-of-the-Gods, King Piyadasi, and is, as it were, another type of revenue.

9. Beloved-of-the-Gods, King Piyadasi, speaks thus: [17] In times of sickness, for the marriage of sons and daughters, at the birth of children, before embarking on a journey, on these and other occasions, people perform various ceremonies. Women in particular perform many vulgar and worthless ceremonies. These types of ceremonies can be performed by all means, but they bear little fruit. What does bear great fruit, however, is the ceremony of the Dhamma. This involves proper behavior towards servants and employees, respect for teachers, restraint towards living beings, and generosity towards ascetics and Brahmans. These and other things constitute the ceremony of the Dhamma. Therefore a father, a son, a brother, a master, a friend, a companion, and even a neighbor should say: "This is good, this is the ceremony that should be performed until its purpose is fulfilled, this I shall do."[18] Other ceremonies are of doubtful fruit, for they may achieve their purpose, or they may not, and even if they do, it is only in this world. But the ceremony of the Dhamma is timeless. Even if it does not achieve its purpose in this world, it produces great merit in the next, whereas if it does achieve its purpose in this world, one gets great merit both here and there through the ceremony of the Dhamma.

10. Beloved-of-the-Gods, King Piyadasi, does not consider glory and fame to be of great account unless they are achieved through having my subjects respect Dhamma and practice Dhamma, both now and in the future.[19] For this alone does Beloved-of-the-Gods, King Piyadasi, desire glory and fame. And whatever efforts Beloved-of-the-Gods, King Piyadasi, is making, all of that is only for the welfare of the people in the next world, and that they will have little evil. And being without merit is evil. This is difficult for either a humble person or a great person to do except with great effort, and by giving up other interests. In fact, it may be even more difficult for a great person to do.

11. Beloved-of-the-Gods, King Piyadasi, speaks thus:[20] There is no gift like the gift of the Dhamma,[21] (no acquaintance like) acquaintance with Dhamma, (no distribution like) distribution of Dhamma, and (no kinship like) kinship through Dhamma. And it consists of this: proper behavior towards servants and employees, respect for mother and father, generosity to friends, companions, relations, Brahmans and ascetics, and not killing living beings. Therefore a father, a son, a brother, a master, a friend, a companion or a neighbor should say: "This is good, this should be done." One benefits in this world and gains great merit in the next by giving the gift of the Dhamma.

12. Beloved-of-the-Gods, King Piyadasi, honors both ascetics and the householders of all religions, and he honors them with gifts and honors of various kinds.[22] But Beloved-of-the-Gods, King Piyadasi, does not value gifts and honors as much as he values this—that there should be growth in the essentials of all religions.[23]

Growth in essentials can be done in different ways, but all of them have as their root restraint in speech, that is, not praising one's own religion, or condemning the religion of others without good cause. And if there is cause for criticism, it should be done in a mild way. But it is better to honor other religions for this reason. By so doing, one's own religion benefits, and so do other religions, while doing otherwise harms one's own religion and the religions of others. Whoever praises his own religion, due to excessive devotion, and condemns others with the thought "Let me glorify my own religion," only harms his own religion. Therefore contact (between religions) is good. [24] One should listen to and respect the doctrines professed by others. Beloved-of-the-Gods, King Piyadasi, desires that all should be well-learned in the good doctrines of other religions.

Those who are content with their own religion should be told this: Beloved-of-the-Gods, King Piyadasi, does not value gifts and honors as much as he values that there should be growth in the essentials of all religions. And to this end many are working—Dhamma Mahamatras, Mahamatras in charge of the women's quarters, officers in charge of outlying areas, and other such officers. And the fruit of this is that one's own religion grows and the Dhamma is illuminated also.

13. Beloved-of-the-Gods, King Piyadasi, conquered the Kalingas eight years after his coronation.[25] One hundred and fifty thousand were deported, one hundred thousand were killed and many more died (from other causes). After the Kalingas had been conquered, Beloved-of-the-Gods came to feel a strong inclination towards the Dhamma, a love for the Dhamma and for instruction in Dhamma. Now Beloved-of-the-Gods feels deep remorse for having conquered the Kalingas.

Indeed, Beloved-of-the-Gods is deeply pained by the killing, dying and deportation that take place when an unconquered country is conquered. But Beloved-of-the-Gods is pained even more by this—that Brahmans, ascetics, and householders of different religions who live in those countries, and who are respectful to superiors, to mother and father, to elders, and who behave properly and have strong loyalty towards friends, acquaintances, companions, relatives, servants and employees—that they are injured, killed or separated from their loved ones. Even those who are not affected (by all this) suffer when they see friends, acquaintances, companions and relatives affected. These misfortunes befall all (as a result of war), and this pains Beloved-of-the-Gods. There is no country, except among the Greeks, where these two groups, Brahmans and ascetics, are not found, and there is no country where people are not devoted to one or another religion.[26] Therefore the killing, death or deportation of a hundredth, or even a thousandth part of those who died during the conquest of Kalinga now pains Beloved-of-the-Gods. Now Beloved-of-the-

Gods thinks that even those who do wrong should be forgiven where forgiveness is possible.

Even the forest people, who live in Beloved-of-the-Gods' domain, are entreated and reasoned with to act properly. They are told that despite his remorse Beloved-of-the-Gods has the power to punish them if necessary, so that they should be ashamed of their wrong and not be killed. Truly, Beloved-of-the-Gods desires non-injury, restraint and impartiality to all beings, even where wrong has been done.

Now it is conquest by Dhamma that Beloved-of-the-Gods considers to be the best conquest.[27] And it (conquest by Dhamma) has been won here, on the borders, even six hundred yojanas away, where the Greek king Antiochos rules, beyond there where the four kings named Ptolemy, Antigonos, Magas and Alexander rule, likewise in the south among the Cholas, the Pandyas, and as far as Tamraparni.[28] Here in the king's domain among the Greeks, the Kambojas, the Nabhakas, the Nabhapamkits, the Bhojas, the Pitinikas, the Andhras and the Palidas, everywhere people are following Beloved-of-the-Gods' instructions in Dhamma. Even where Beloved-of-the-Gods' envoys have not been, these people too, having heard of the practice of Dhamma and the ordinances and instructions in Dhamma given by Beloved-of-the-Gods, are following it and will continue to do so. This conquest has been won everywhere, and it gives great joy—the joy which only conquest by Dhamma can give. But even this joy is of little consequence. Beloved-of-the-Gods considers the great fruit to be experienced in the next world to be more important.

I have had this Dhamma edict written so that my sons and great-grandsons may not consider making new conquests, or that if military conquests are made, that they be done with forbearance and light punishment, or better still, that they consider making conquest by Dhamma only, for that bears fruit in this world and the next. May all their intense devotion be given to this which has a result in this world and the next.

14. Beloved-of-the-Gods, King Piyadasi, has had these Dhamma edicts written in brief, in medium length, and in extended form.[29] Not all of them occur everywhere, for my domain is vast, but much has been written, and I will have still more written. And also there are some subjects here that have been spoken of again and again because of their sweetness, and so that the people may act in accordance with them. If some things written are incomplete, this is because of the locality, or in consideration of the object, or due to the fault of the scribe.

Kama Sutra

Man, the period of whose life is one hundred years, should practice Dharma, Artha and Kama at different times and in such a manner that they may harmonize together and not clash in any way … Dharma is obedience to the command of the Shastra (Holy Writ of the Hindus to do certain things, such as the performance of sacrifices). Artha is the acquisition of arts, land, gold, cattle, wealth and friends. Kama is the enjoyment of appropriate objects by the five senses of hearing, feeling, seeing, tasting and smelling, assisted by the mind together with the soul. The ingredient in this is a peculiar contact between the organ of sense and its object, and the consciousness of pleasure which arises from that contact is called Kama. Kama is to be learnt from the Kama Sutra (aphorisms on love or science of love) and from the practice of citizens.

ON KISSING

It is said by some that there is no fixed time or order between the embrace, the kiss, and the pressing or scratching with the nails or fingers, but that all these things should be done generally before sexual union takes place, while striking and making the various sounds generally takes place at the time of union. Vatsyayana, however, thinks that anything may take place at any time, for love does not care for time or order. On the occasion of the first congress (meeting), kissing and the other things mentioned above should be done moderately, they should not be continued for a long time, and should be done alternately. On subsequent occasions however the reverse of all this may take place, and moderation will not be necessary, they may continue for a long time and for the purpose of kindling love, they may all be done at the same time.

The following are the places for kissing: the forehead, the eyes, the cheeks, the throat, the bosom, the breasts, the lips, and the interior of the mouth. Moreover, the people of the Lat country kiss also the following places: the joints, the thighs, the arms, and the navel. But Vatsyayana thinks that though kissing is practiced by these people in the above places on account of the intensity of their love, and the customs of their country, it is not fit to be practiced by all.

HOMER'S *ILIAD*
THE WRATH OF ACHILLEUS

TRANSLATED BY GEORGE ERNLE

London 1922

I

Sing me that Anger, Goddess, which blinding royal Achilleus
Balefully, brought sufferings untold to the army of Argos,
Sent many souls of mighty Achaeans into the darkness
And flung abroad the bodies to the wild dogs and to the vultures
And to the fowls of Heaven, till Zeus had duly accomplished
All he decreed. Sing of it from where Agamemnon Atrides
And the gallant Achileus first fought and parted asunder.
What God aroused contention amongst these so to divide them?
"Twas the son of Cronides and Leto. He in his anger
Sent Agamemnon's army a foul plague, and the Achaeans   10

Lay ever dying of it; for why, Agamemnon Atrides
Shamefully used Chryses, God's priest, when bearing enormous
Wealth to redeem his daughter, he ventured unto the swift ships,
And carrying the fillets of a priest of Phoebus Apollon,
Bound on a golden scepter, besought the Achaean Assembly,
Turning him especially to the two Kings, children of Atreus.
    "Ye Sovereigns and people of Argos, may the eternal
God, dwelling in the Heavens, vouchsafe your army to conquer

Priamos and carry home your spoil to the country you came from:
Only allow my daughter to go free, taking an ample   20

Price for her, and reverence God's son, far-darting Apollon."
    With one a accord the remaining Achaeans bade Agamemnon
Show the prophet reverence and take so noble a ransom,
How so this pleased not their lord Agamemnon Atrides,
And he reviled and drove him away and rudely denied him.
    "Quit my sight, graybeard, and do not let me behold you
    Loitering or coming here henceforward unto the warships,
    Lest chaplets and scepter avail no longer to save you.
    I"ll never free your daughter. The years shall find her in Argos,
    Find her a slave dwelling in my halls far over the water,   30
Pacing at her loom there and sleeping nightly beside me,
    So disappear, and quickly, before I do you a mischief
    Such was Atrides' answer. The old man trembling obey'd him,
Pass'd from him in silence by plunging thunderous Ocean,
And when alone, uplifted his old voice, crying in anguish
 On the son of bright-hair'd Leto, King Phoebos Apollon.
    "Lord o" the Bow of Silver, who art as a tower to Chryse,
Guarding us, and rulest Tenedos with mighty dominion,
Smintheus, hear and help me! If I have builded a gracious
Temple,—if I offer up fat goats and slaughter the choicest   40
Bulls in it, oh suffer this my boon to be duly accomplish'd;
Smite the Achaean people,—avenge my weeping upon them."
    So he besought. His prayer was heard by Phoebos Apollon,
And he descended lofty Olympus, flaming in anger,
His quiver fill'd with arrows, his bow on shoulder behind him:
And the arrows range again for his heart's wrath, rattling at every
Stride of him. Invisibly, as night falls, so he descended,
And sat apart, looking over the warships of the Achaeans,
Whence as he loosed the arrow, his bow clang'd, evilly sounding.
First Phoebos smote only the mules and sharp-eyed watchdogs,   50
But very soon turn'd unto the men's selves, loosing his awful
 Archery; and bodies of dead men burn'd numberless alway.

Pre-Socratic Philosophy
Early Greek Thought
(5th Century BCE)

THE FRAGMENTS OF ANAXIMANDER

1. "Immortal and indestructible," "surrounds all and directs all."
2. "(To that they return when they are destroyed) of necessity; for he says that they suffer punishment and give satisfaction to one another for injustice."

ANAXAGORAS

(1) All things were together, infinite both in number and in smallness; for the small too was infinite. And, when all things were together, none of them could be distinguished for their smallness. For air and aether prevailed over all things, being both of them infinite; for amongst all things these are the greatest both in quantity and size.

(2) For air and aether are separated off from the mass that surrounds the world, and the surrounding mass is infinite in quantity.

(3) Nor is there a least of what is small, but there is always a smaller; for it cannot be that what is should cease to be by being cut. But there is also always something greater than what is great, and it is equal to the small in amount, and, compared with itself, each thing is both great and small.

(4) And since these things are so, we must suppose that there are contained many things and of all sorts in the things that are uniting, seeds of all things, with all sorts of

shapes and colors and savors and that men have been formed in them, and the other animals that have life, and that these men have inhabited cities and cultivated fields as with us; and that they have a sun and a moon and the rest as with us; and that their earth brings forth for them many things of all kinds of which they gather the best together into their dwellings, and use them. Thus much have I said with regard to separating off, to show that it will not be only with us that things are separated off, but elsewhere too.

But before they were separated off, when all things were together, not even was any color distinguishable; for the mixture of all things prevented it—of the moist and the dry; and the warm and the cold, and the light and the dark, and of much earth that was in it, and of a multitude of innumerable seeds in no way like each, other. For none of the other things either is like any other. And these things being so, we must hold that all things are in the whole.

(5) And those things having been thus decided, we must know that all of them are neither more nor less; for it is not possible for them to be more than all, and all are always equal.

(6) And since the portions of the great and of the small are equal in amount, for this reason, too, all things will be in everything; nor is it possible for them to be apart, but all things have a portion of everything. Since it is impossible for there to be a least thing, they cannot be separated, nor come to be by themselves; but they must be now, just as they were in the beginning, all-together. And in all things many things are contained, and an equal number both in the greater and in the smaller of the things that are separated off.

(7) … So that we cannot know the number of the things that are separated off, either in word or deed.

(8) The things that are in one world are not divided nor cut off from one another with a hatchet, neither the warm from the cold nor the cold from the warm.

(9) … as these things revolve and are separated off by the force and swiftness. And the swiftness makes the force. Their swiftness is not like the swiftness of any of the things that are now among men, but in every way many times as swift.

(10) How can hair come from what is not hair, or flesh from what is not flesh?

(11) In everything there is a portion of everything except Nous, and there are some things in which there is Nous also.

(12) All other things partake in a portion of everything, while Nous is infinite and self-ruled, and is mixed with nothing, but is alone itself by itself. For if it were not by itself, but were mixed with anything else, it would partake in all things if it were mixed with any; for in everything there is a portion of everything, as has been said by me in what goes before, and the things mixed with it would hinder it, so that it would have power over nothing in the same way that it has now being alone by itself. For it is the thinnest of all things and the purest, and it has all knowledge

about everything and the greatest strength; and Nous has power over all things, both greater and smaller, that have life. And Nous had power over the whole revolution, so that it began to revolve in the beginning. And it began to revolve first from a small beginning; but the revolution now extends over a larger space, and will extend over a larger still. And all the things that are mingled together and separated off and distinguished are all known by Nous. And Nous set in order all things that were to be, and all things that were and are not now and that are, and this revolution in which now revolve the stars and the sun and the moon, and the air and the aether that are separated off. And this revolution caused the separating off, and the rare is separated off from the dense, the warm from the cold, the light from the dark, and the dry from the moist. And there are many portions in many things. But no thing is altogether separated off nor distinguished from anything else except Nous. And all Nous is alike, both the greater and the smaller; while nothing else is like anything else, but each single thing is and was most manifestly those things of which if has most in it.

(13)   And when Nous began to move things, separating off took place from all that was moved, and so much as Nous set in motion was separated. And as things were set in motion and separated, the revolution caused them to be separated much more.

(14)   And Nous, which ever is, is certainly there, where everything else is, in the surrounding mass, and in what has been united with it and separated off from it.

(15)   The dense and the moist and the cold and the dark came together where the earth is now, while the rare and the warm and the dry (and the bright) went out towards the further part of the aether.

(16)   From these as they are separated off earth is solidified; for from mists water is separated off, and from water earth. From the earth stones are solidified by the cold, and these rush outwards more than water.

(17)   The Hellenes follow a wrong usage in speaking of coming into being and passing away; for nothing comes into being or passes away, but there is mingling and separation of things that are. So they would be right to call coming into being mixture, and passing away separation.

(18)   It is the sun that puts brightness into the moon.

(19)   We call rainbow the reflexion of the sun in the clouds. Now it is a sign of storm; for the water that flows round the cloud causes wind or pours down in rain.

(20)   With the rise of the Dogstar (?) men begin the harvest; with its setting they begin to till the fields. It is hidden for forty days and nights.

(21)   From the weakness of our senses we are not able to judge the truth.

(21a) What appears is a vision of the unseen.

(21b) (We can make use of the lower animals) because we use our own experience and memory and wisdom and art.

(22)   What is called "birds' milk" is the white of the egg.

PLUTARCH

LIFE OF LYCURGUS 14–16

PLUTARCH.

For the good education of their youth, he (Lycurgus) went so far back as to take into consideration their very conception and birth, by regulating their marriages. For Aristotle is wrong in saying, that, after he had tried all ways for reduce the women to more modesty and sobriety, he was at last forced to leave them as they were, because that in the absence of their husbands, who spent the best part of their lives in the wars, their wives, whom they were obliged to leave absolute mistresses at home, took great liberties and assumed the superiority; and were treated with overmuch respect and called by the title of lady or queen. The truth is, he took in their case, also, all the care that was possible; he ordered the maidens to exercise themselves with wrestling, running, throwing the javelin, and casting the dart, to the end that the fruit they conceived might, in strong and healthy bodies, take firmer root and find better growth, and withal that they, with their greater vigor, might be the more able to undergo the pains of child-bearing … These public processions of the maidens, and their appearing naked in their exercises and dancing, were incitements to marriage, operation upon the young with the rigor and certainty, as Plato says, of love, if not of mathematics.

ii. Plutarch, Sayings of Spartan Women:

Being asked by a woman from Attica, "Why is it that you Spartan women are the only women that lord it over your men," [one woman] said, "Because we are the only women that are mothers of men.

ATHENIAN WOMEN:

"We have prostitutes [hetairai] for the sake of pleasure, concubines for daily care of the body, and wives for the purpose of begetting legitimate children and having a reliable guardian of the contents of the house."

Artistotle, Politics:

The freeman rules over the slave after another manner from that in which the male rules over the female, or the man over the child; although the parts of the soul are present in all of them, they are present in different degrees. For the slave has not deliberative faculty at all; the woman has, but it is without authority, and the child has, but it is immature … Clearly, then moral virtue belongs to all of them; but the temperance of a man and of a woman, or the courage and justice of a man and of a woman, are not, as Socrates maintained, the same; the courage of a man is shown in commanding, of a woman in obeying … All classes must be deemed to have their special attributes; as the poet says of women, "silence is a woman's glory," but this is not equally the glory of man.

THE BATTLE OF PLATEA (479 BCE)
HERODOTUS BOOK IX

All these, except the Helots—seven of whom, as I said, attended each Spartan—were heavy-armed troops; and they amounted to thirty-eight thousand seven hundred men. This was the number of Hoplites, or heavy-armed soldiers, which was together against the barbarian. The light-armed troops consisted of the thirty-five thousand ranged with the Spartans, seven in attendance upon each, who were all well equipped for war; and of thirty-four thousand five hundred others, belonging to the Lacedaemonians and the rest of the Greeks, at the rate (nearly) of one light to one heavy armed. Thus the entire number of the light-armed was sixty-nine thousand five hundred.

The Greek army, therefore, which mustered at Plataea, counting light-armed as well as heavy-armed, was but eighteen hundred men short of one hundred and ten thousand; and this amount was exactly made up by the Thespians who were present in the camp; for eighteen hundred Thespians, being the whole number left, were likewise with the army; but these men were without arms. Such was the array of the Greek troops when they took post on the Asopus.

The barbarians under Mardonius, when the mourning for Masistius was at an end, and they learnt that the Greeks were in the Plataean territory, moved likewise towards the river Asopus, which flows in those parts. On their arrival Mardonius marshalled them against the Greeks in the following order:—Against the Lacedaemonians he posted his Persians; and as the Persians were far more numerous he drew them up with their ranks deeper than common, and also extended their front so that part faced the Tegeans; and here he took care to choose out the best troops to face the Lacedaemonians, whilst against the

Herodotus, *The History of Herodotus*, Book IX, trans. George Rawlinson. Copyright in the Public Domain.

Tegeans he arrayed those on whom he could not so much depend. This was done at the suggestion and by the advice of the Thebans. Next to the Persians he placed the Medes, facing the Corinthians, Potidaeans, Orchomenians, and Sicyonians; then the Bactrians, facing the Epidaurians, Troezenians, Lepreats, Tirynthians, Mycenaeans, and Phliasians; after them the Indians, facing the Hermionians, Eretrians, Styreans, and Chalcidians; then the Sacans, facing the Ambraciots, Anactorians, Leucadians, Paleans, and Eginetans; last of all, facing the Athenians, the Plataeans, and the Megarians, he placed the troops of the Boeotians, Locrians, Malians, and Thessalians, and also the thousand Phocians. The whole nation of the Phocians had not joined the Medes; on the contrary, there were some who had gathered themselves into bands about Parnassus, and made expeditions from thence, whereby they distressed Mardonius and the Greeks who sided with him, and so did good service to the Grecian cause. Besides those mentioned above, Mardonius likewise arrayed against the Athenians the Macedonians and the tribes dwelling about Thessaly.

I have named here the greatest of the nations which were marshalled by Mardonius on this occasion, to wit, all those of most renown and account. Mixed with these, however, were men of divers other peoples, as Phrygians, Thracians, Mysians, Paeonians, and the like; Ethiopians again, and Egyptians, both of the Hermotybian and Calascirian races, whose weapon is the sword, and who are the only fighting men in that country. These persons had formerly served on board the fleet of Xerxes, but Mardonius disembarked them before he left Phalerum; in the land force which Xerxes brought to Athens there were no Egyptians. The number of the barbarians, as I have already mentioned, was three hundred thousand; that of the Greeks who had made alliance with Mardonius is known to none, for they were never counted: I should guess that they mustered near fifty thousand strong. The troops thus marshalled were all foot soldiers. As for the horse, it was drawn up by itself.

When the marshalling of Mardonius' troops by nations and by maniples was ended, the two armies proceeded on the next day to offer sacrifice. The Grecian sacrifice was offered by Tisamenus, the son of Antiochus, who accompanied the army as soothsayer: he was an Elean, and belonged to the Clytiad branch of the Iamidae, but had been admitted among their own citizens by the Lacedaemonians. Now his admission among them was on this wise:—Tisamenus had gone to Delphi to consult the god concerning his lack of offspring, when it was declared to him by the Pythoness that he would win five very glorious combats. Misunderstanding the oracle, and imagining that he was to win combats in the games, Tisamenus at once applied himself to the practice of gymnastics. He trained himself for the Pentathlum, and, on contending at Olympia, came within a little of winning it; for he was successful in everything, except the wrestling-match, which was carried off by Hieronymus the Andrian. Hereon the Lacedaemonians perceived that the combats of which the oracle spoke were not combats in the games, but battles: they therefore sought to induce Tisamenus to hire out his services to them, in order that they might join him with their Heracleid kings in the conduct of their wars. He however, when he saw that they set great store by his friendship, forthwith raised his price, and told them, "If they would receive him among their citizens, and give him equal rights with the rest, he was willing to do as they desired, but on no other terms would they ever gain his consent." The Spartans, when they heard this, at first thought it monstrous, and ceased to implore his aid. Afterwards, however, when the fearful danger of the Persian war hung over their heads, they sent for him and agreed to his terms; but Tisamenus now, perceiving them so changed, declared, "He could no longer be content with what he had asked before: they must likewise make his brother Hagias a Spartan, with the same rights as himself."

In acting thus he did but follow the example once set by Melampus, at least if kingship may be compared with citizenship. For when the women of Argos were seized with madness, and the Argives would have hired Melampus to come from Pylos and heal them of their disease, he demanded as his reward one-half of the kingdom; but as the Argives disdained to stoop to this, they left him and went their way. Afterwards, however, when many more of their women were seized, they brought themselves to agree to his terms; and accordingly they went again to him, and said they were content to give what he required. Hereon Melampus, seeing them so changed, raised his demand, and told them, "Except they would give his brother Bias one-third of the kingdom likewise, he would not do as they wished." So, as the Argives were in a strait, they consented even to this.

In like manner the Spartans, as they were in great need of Tisamenus, yielded everything: and Tisamenus the Elean, having in this way become a Spartan citizen, afterwards, in the capacity of soothsayer, helped the Spartans to gain five very glorious combats. He and his brother were the only men whom the Spartans ever admitted to citizenship. The five combats were these following:—The first was the combat at Plataea; the second, that near Tegea, against the Tegeans and the Argives; the third, that at Dipaeeis, against all the Arcadians excepting those of Mantinea; the fourth, that at the Isthmus, against the Messenians; and the fifth, that at Tanagra, against the Athenians and the Argives. The battle here fought was the last of all the five.

The Spartans had now brought Tisamenus with them to the Plataean territory, where he acted as soothsayer for the Greeks. He found the victims favourable, if the Greeks stood on the defensive, but not if they began the battle or crossed the river Asopus.

With Mardonius also, who was very eager to begin the battle, the victims were not favourable for so doing; but he likewise found them bode him well, if he was content to stand on his defence. He too had made use of the Grecian rites; for Hegesistratus, an Elean, and the most renowned of the Telliads, was his soothsayer. This man had once been taken captive by the Spartans, who, considering that he had done them many grievous injuries, laid him in bonds, with the intent to put him to death. Thereupon Hegesistratus, finding himself in so sore a case, since not only was his life in danger, but he knew that he would have to suffer torments of many kinds before his death,—Hegesistratus, I say, did a deed for which no words suffice. He had been set with one foot in the stocks, which were of wood but bound with iron bands; and in this condition received from without an iron implement, wherewith he contrived to accomplish the most courageous deed upon record. Calculating how much of his foot he would be able to draw through the hole, he cut off the front portion with his own hand; and then, as he was guarded by watchmen, forced a way through the wall of his prison, and made his escape to Tegea, travelling during the night, but in the daytime stealing into the woods, and staying there. In this way, though the Lacedaemonians went out in full force to search for him, he nevertheless escaped, and arrived the third evening at Tegea. So the Spartans were amazed at the man's endurance, when they saw on the ground the piece which he had cut off his foot, and yet for all their seeking could not find him anywhere. Hegesistratus, having thus escaped the Lacedaemonians, took refuge in Tegea; for the Tegeans at that time were ill friends with the Lacedaemonians. When his wound was healed, he procured himself a wooden foot, and became an open enemy to Sparta. At the last, however, this enmity brought him to trouble; for the Spartans took him captive as he was exercising his office in Zacynthus, and forthwith put him to death. But these things happened some while after the fight at Plataea. At present he was serving Mardonius on the Asopus, having been hired at no inconsiderable price; and here he offered sacrifice with a right good will, in part from his hatred of the Lacedaemonians, in part for lucre's sake.

So when the victims did not allow either the Persians or their Greek allies to begin the battle—these Greeks had their own soothsayer in the person of Hippomachus, a Leucadian—and when soldiers continued to pour into the opposite camp and the numbers on the Greek side to increase continually, Timagenidas, the son of Herpys, a Theban, advised Mardonius to keep a watch on the passes of Cithaeron, telling him how supplies of men kept flocking in day after day, and assuring him that he might cut off large numbers.

It was eight days after the two armies first encamped opposite to one another when this advice was given by Timagenidas. Mardonius, seeing it to be good, as soon as evening came, sent his cavalry to that pass of Mount Cithaeron which opens out upon Plataea, a pass called by the Boeotians the "Three Heads," called the "Oak-Heads" by the Athenians. The horse sent on this errand did not make the movement in vain. They came upon a body of five hundred sumpter-beasts which were just entering the plain, bringing provisions to the Greek camp from the Peloponnese, with a number of men driving them. Seeing this prey in their power, the Persians set upon them and slaughtered them, sparing none, neither man nor beast; till at last, when they had had enough of slaying, they secured such as were left, and bore them off to the camp to Mardonius.

After this they waited again for two days more, neither army wishing to begin the fight. The barbarians indeed advanced as far as the Asopus, and endeavoured to tempt the Greeks to cross; but neither side actually passed the stream. Still the cavalry of Mardonius harassed and annoyed the Greeks incessantly; for the Thebans, who were zealous in the cause of the Medes, pressed the war forward with all eagerness, and often led the charge till the lines met, when the Medes and Persians took their place, and displayed, many of them, uncommon valour.

For ten days nothing was done more than this; but on the eleventh day from the time when the two hosts first took station, one over against the other, near Plataea—the number of the Greeks being now much greater than it was at the first, and Mardonius being impatient of the delay—there was a conference held between Mardonius, son of Gobryas, and Artabazus, son of Pharnaces, a man who was esteemed by Xerxes more than almost any of the Persians. At this consultation the following were the opinions delivered:—Artabazus thought it would be best for them to break up from their quarters as soon as possible, and withdraw the whole army to the fortified town of Thebes, where they had abundant stores of corn for themselves, and of fodder for the sumpter-beasts. There, he said, they had only to sit quiet, and the war might be brought to an end on this wise:—Coined gold was plentiful in the camp, and uncoined gold too; they had silver moreover in great abundance, and drinking-cups. Let them not spare to take of these, and distribute them among the Greeks, especially among the leaders in the several cities; "would not be long before the Greeks gave up their liberty, without risking another battle for it. Thus the opinion of Artabazus agreed with that of the Thebans; for he too had more foresight than some. Mardonius, on the other hand, expressed himself with more fierceness and obstinacy, and was utterly disinclined to yield. "Their army," he said, "was vastly superior to that of the Greeks; and they had best engage at once, and not wait till greater numbers were gathered against them. As for Hegesistratus and his victims, they should let them pass unheeded, not seeking to force them to be favourable, but, according to the old Persian custom, hasting to join battle."

PERICLES'S FUNERAL ORATION

Most of my predecessors in this place have commended him who made this speech part of the law, telling us that it is well that it should be delivered at the burial of those who fall in battle. For myself, I should have thought that the worth which had displayed itself in deeds would be sufficiently rewarded by honours also shown by deeds, such as you now see in this funeral prepared at the people's cost. And I could have wished that the reputations of many brave men were not to be imperilled in the mouth of a single individual, to stand or fall according as he spoke well or ill. For it is hard to speak properly upon a subject where it is even difficult to convince your hearers that you are speaking the truth. On the one hand, the friend who is familiar with every fact of the story may think that some point has not been set forth with that fullness which he wishes and knows it to deserve; on the other, he who is a stranger to the matter may be led by envy to suspect exaggeration if he hears anything above his own nature. For men can endure to hear others praised only so long as they can severally persuade themselves of their own ability to equal the actions recounted: when this point is passed, envy comes in and with it incredulity. However, since our ancestors have stamped this custom with their approval, it becomes my duty to obey the law and to try to satisfy your several wishes and opinions as best I may.

I shall begin with our ancestors: it is both just and proper that they should have the honour of the first mention on an occasion like the present. They dwelt in the country without break in the succession from generation to generation, and handed it down free to the present time by their valour. And if our more remote ancestors deserve praise,

Thucydides, *History of the Peloponnesian War*, trans. Richard Crawley. Copyright in the Public Domain.

much more do our own fathers, who added to their inheritance the empire which we now possess, and spared no pains to be able to leave their acquisitions to us of the present generation. Lastly, there are few parts of our dominions that have not been augmented by those of us here, who are still more or less in the vigour of life; while the mother country has been furnished by us with everything that can enable her to depend on her own resources whether for war or for peace. That part of our history which tells of the military achievements which gave us our several possessions, or of the ready valour with which either we or our fathers stemmed the tide of Hellenic or foreign aggression, is a theme too familiar to my hearers for me to dilate on, and I shall therefore pass it by. But what was the road by which we reached our position, what the form of government under which our greatness grew, what the national habits out of which it sprang; these are questions which I may try to solve before I proceed to my panegyric upon these men; since I think this to be a subject upon which on the present occasion a speaker may properly dwell, and to which the whole assemblage, whether citizens or foreigners, may listen with advantage.

"Our constitution does not copy the laws of neighbouring states; we are rather a pattern to others than imitators ourselves. Its administration favours the many instead of the few; this is why it is called a democracy. If we look to the laws, they afford equal justice to all in their private differences; if no social standing, advancement in public life falls to reputation for capacity, class considerations not being allowed to interfere with merit; nor again does poverty bar the way, if a man is able to serve the state, he is not hindered by the obscurity of his condition. The freedom which we enjoy in our government extends also to our ordinary life. There, far from exercising a jealous surveillance over each other, we do not feel called upon to be angry with our neighbour for doing what he likes, or even to indulge in those injurious looks which cannot fail to be offensive, although they inflict no positive penalty. But all this ease in our private relations does not make us lawless as citizens. Against this fear is our chief safeguard, teaching us to obey the magistrates and the laws, particularly such as regard the protection of the injured, whether they are actually on the statute book or belong to that code which, although unwritten, yet cannot be broken without acknowledged disgrace.

"Further, we provide plenty of means for the mind to refresh itself from business. We celebrate games and sacrifices all the year round, and the elegance of our private establishments forms a daily source of pleasure and helps to banish the spleen; while the magnitude of our city draws the produce of the world into our harbour, so that to the Athenian the fruits of other countries are as familiar a luxury as those of his own.

"If we turn to our military policy, there also we differ from our antagonists. We throw open our city to the world, and never by alien acts exclude foreigners from any opportunity of learning or observing, although the eyes of an enemy may occasionally profit by our liberality; trusting less in system and policy than to the native spirit of our citizens; while in education, where our rivals from their very cradles by a painful discipline seek after manliness, at Athens we live exactly as we please, and yet are just as ready to encounter every legitimate danger. In proof of this it may be noticed that the Lacedaemonians do not invade our country alone, but bring with them all their confederates; while we Athenians advance unsupported into the territory of a neighbour, and fighting upon a foreign soil usually vanquish with ease men who are defending their homes. Our united force was never yet encountered by any enemy, because we have at once to attend to our marine and to dispatch our citizens by land upon a hundred different services; so that, wherever they engage with some such fraction of our strength, a success against a detachment is magnified into a victory over the nation, and a defeat into a reverse suffered at the hands of our entire people. And yet if with habits not of labour but of ease, and courage not of art but of nature, we are still willing to encounter danger, we have the double advantage of escaping the experience of hardships in anticipation and of facing them in the hour of need as fearlessly as those who are never free from them.

"Nor are these the only points in which our city is worthy of admiration. We cultivate refinement without extravagance and knowledge without effeminacy; wealth we employ more for use than for show, and place the real disgrace of poverty not in owning to the fact but in declining the struggle against it. Our public men have, besides politics, their private affairs to attend to, and our ordinary citizens, though occupied with the pursuits of industry, are still fair judges of public matters; for, unlike any other nation, regarding him who takes no part in these duties not as unambitious but as useless, we Athenians are able to judge at all events if we cannot originate, and, instead of looking on discussion as a stumbling-block in the way of action, we think it an indispensable preliminary to any wise action at all. Again, in our enterprises we present the singular spectacle of daring and deliberation, each carried to its highest point, and both united in the same persons; although usually decision is the fruit of ignorance, hesitation of reflection. But the palm of courage will surely be adjudged most justly to those who best know the difference between hardship and pleasure and yet are never tempted to shrink from danger. In generosity we are equally singular, acquiring our friends by conferring, not by receiving, favours. Yet, of course, the doer of the favour is the firmer friend of the two, in order by continued kindness to keep the recipient in his debt; while the debtor feels less keenly from the very consciousness that the return he makes will be a payment, not a free gift. And it is only the Athenians who, fearless of consequences, confer their benefits not from calculations of expediency, but in the confidence of liberality.

In short, I say that as a city we are the school of Hellas, while I doubt if the world can produce a man who, where he has only himself to depend upon, is equal to so many emergencies, and graced by so happy a versatility, as the Athenian. And that this is no mere boast thrown out for the occasion, but plain matter of fact, the power of the state acquired by these habits proves. For Athens alone of her contemporaries is found when tested to be greater than her reputation, and alone gives no occasion to her assailants to blush at the antagonist by whom they have been worsted, or to her subjects to question her title by merit to rule. Rather, the admiration of the present and succeeding ages will be ours, since we have not left our power without witness, but have shown it by mighty proofs; and far from needing a Homer for our panegyrist, or other of his craft whose verses might charm for the moment only for the impression which they gave to melt at the touch of fact, we have forced every sea and land to be the highway of our daring, and everywhere, whether for evil or for good, have left imperishable monuments behind us. Such is the Athens for which these men, in the assertion of their resolve not to lose her, nobly fought and died; and well may every one of their survivors be ready to suffer in her cause.

Indeed if I have dwelt at some length upon the character of our country, it has been to show that our stake in the struggle is not the same as theirs who have no such blessings to lose, and also that the panegyric of the men over whom I am now speaking might be by definite proofs established. That panegyric is now in a great measure complete; for the Athens that I have celebrated is only what the heroism of these and their like have made her, men whose fame, unlike that of most Hellenes, will be found to be only commensurate with their deserts. And if a test of worth be wanted, it is to be found in their closing scene, and this not only in cases in which it set the final seal upon their merit, but also in those in which it gave the first intimation of their having any. For there is justice in the claim that steadfastness in his country's battles should be as a cloak to cover a man's other imperfections; since the good action has blotted out the bad, and his merit as a citizen more than outweighed his demerits as an individual. But none of these allowed either wealth with its prospect of future enjoyment to unnerve his spirit, or poverty with its hope of a day of freedom and riches to tempt him to shrink from danger. No, holding that vengeance upon their enemies was more to be desired than any personal blessings, and reckoning this to be the most glorious of hazards, they joyfully determined to accept the risk, to make sure of their vengeance, and to let their wishes wait; and while committing to hope the uncertainty of final success, in the business before them they thought fit to act boldly and trust in themselves. Thus choosing to die resisting, rather than to live submitting, they fled only from dishonour, but met danger face to face, and after one brief moment, while at the summit of their fortune, escaped, not from their fear, but from their glory.

So died these men as became Athenians. You, their survivors, must determine to have as unfaltering a resolution in the field, though you may pray that it may have a happier issue. And not contented with ideas derived only from words of the advantages which are bound up with the defence of your country, though these would furnish a valuable text to a speaker even before an audience so alive to them as the present, you must yourselves realize the power of Athens, and feed your eyes upon her from day to day, till love of her fills your hearts; and then, when all her greatness shall break upon you, you must reflect that it was by courage, sense of duty, and a keen feeling of honour in action that men were enabled to win all this, and that no personal failure in an enterprise could make them consent to deprive their country of their valour, but they laid it at her feet as the most glorious contribution that they could offer. For this offering of their lives made in common by them all they each of them individually received that renown which never grows old, and for a sepulchre, not so much that in which their bones have been deposited, but that noblest of shrines wherein their glory is laid up to be eternally remembered upon every occasion on which deed or story shall call for its commemoration. For heroes have the whole earth for their tomb; and in lands far from their own, where the column with its epitaph declares it, there is enshrined in every breast a record unwritten with no tablet to preserve it, except that of the heart. These take as your model and, judging happiness to be the fruit of freedom and freedom of valour, never decline the dangers of war. For it is not the miserable that would most justly be unsparing of their lives; these have nothing to hope for: it is rather they to whom continued life may bring reverses as yet unknown, and to whom a fall, if it came, would be most tremendous in its consequences. And surely, to a man of spirit, the degradation of cowardice must be immeasurably more grievous than the unfelt death which strikes him in the midst of his strength and patriotism!

"Comfort, therefore, not condolence, is what I have to offer to the parents of the dead who may be here. Numberless are the chances to which, as they know, the life of man is subject; but fortunate indeed are they who draw for their lot a death so glorious as that which has caused your mourning, and to whom life has been so exactly measured as to terminate in the happiness in which it has been passed. Still I know that this is a hard saying, especially when those are in question of whom you will constantly be reminded by seeing in the homes of others blessings of which once you also boasted: for grief is felt not so much for the want of what we have never known, as for the loss of that to which we have been long accustomed. Yet you who are still of an age to beget children must bear up in the hope of having others in their stead; not only will they help you to forget those whom you have lost, but will be to the state at once a reinforcement and a security; for never can a fair or just policy be expected of the citizen who does not, like his fellows, bring to the decision the interests and apprehensions of a father. While those of you who have passed your prime must congratulate yourselves with the thought that the best part of your life was fortunate, and that the brief span that remains will be cheered by the fame of the departed. For it is only the love of honour that never grows old; and honour it is, not gain, as some would have it, that rejoices the heart of age and helplessness.

"Turning to the sons or brothers of the dead, I see an arduous struggle before you. When a man is gone, all are wont to praise him, and should your merit be ever so transcendent, you will still find it difficult not merely to overtake, but even to approach their renown. The living have envy to contend with, while those who are no longer in our path are honoured with a goodwill into which rivalry does not enter. On the other hand, if I must say anything on the subject of female excellence to those of you who will now be in widowhood, it will be all comprised in this brief exhortation. Great will be your glory in not falling short of your natural character; and greatest will be hers who is least talked of among the men, whether for good or for bad.

"My task is now finished. I have performed it to the best of my ability, and in word, at least, the requirements of the law are now satisfied. If deeds be in question, those who are here interred have received part of their honours already, and for the rest, their children will be brought up till manhood at the public expense: the state thus offers a valuable prize, as the garland of victory in this race of valour, for the reward both of those who have fallen and their survivors. And where the rewards for merit are greatest, there are found the best citizens.

"And now that you have brought to a close your lamentations for your relatives, you may depart."

ALEXANDER THE GREAT
IN PERSIA ARRIAN ANABASIS OF ALEXANDER, BOOK VII

1. When Alexander arrived at Pasargadae and Persepolis, he was seized with an ardent desire to sail down the Euphrates and Tigris to the Persian Sea, and to see the mouths of those rivers as he had already seen those of the Indus as well as the sea into which it flows. Some authors also have stated that he was meditating a voyage round the larger portion of Arabia, the country of the Ethiopians, Libya, and Numidia beyond Mount Atlas to Gadeira, inward into our sea; thinking that after he had subdued both Libya and Carchedon, then indeed he might with justice be called king of all Asia. For he said that the kings of the Persians and Medes called themselves Great Kings without any right, since they ruled a comparatively small part of Asia. Some say that he was meditating a voyage thence into the Euxine Sea, to Scythia and the Lake Maeotis; while others assert that he intended to go to Sicily and the Iapygian Cape, for the fame of the Romans spreading far and wide was now exciting his jealousy. For my own part I cannot conjecture with any certainty what were his plans; and I do not care to guess. But this I think I can confidently affirm, that he meditated nothing small or mean; and that he would never have remained satisfied with any of the acquisitions he had made, even if he had added Europe to Asia, or the islands of the Britons to Europe; but would still have gone on seeking for some unknown land beyond those mentioned. I verily believe that if he had found no one else to strive with, he would have striven with himself …

4. In Susa, he celebrated both his own wedding and those of his companions. He himself married Barsine, the eldest daughter of Darius, and according to Aristobulus,

besides her another, Parysatis, the youngest daughter of Ochus. He had already married Roxana, daughter of Oxyartes the Bactrian. To Hephaestion he gave Drypetis, another daughter of Darius, and his own wife's sister; for he wished Hephaestion's children to be first cousins to his own. To Craterus he gave Amastrine, daughter of Oxyartes the brother of Darius; to Perdiccas, the daughter of Atropates, viceroy of Media; to Ptolemy the confidential body-guard, and Eumenes the royal secretary, the daughters of Artabazus, to the former Artacama, and to the latter Artonis. To Nearchus he gave the daughter of Barsine and Mentor; to Seleucus the daughter of Spitamenes the Bactrian. Likewise to the rest of his Companions he gave the choicest daughters of the Persians and Medes, to the number of eighty. The weddings were celebrated after the Persian manner, seats being placed in a row for the bridegrooms; and after the banquet the brides came in and seated themselves, each one near her own husband. The bridegrooms took them by the right hand and kissed them; the king being the first to begin, for the weddings of all were conducted in the same way. This appeared the most popular thing which Alexander ever did; and it proved his affection for his Companions. Each man took his own bride and led her away; and on all without exception Alexander bestowed doweries, He also ordered that the names of all the other Macedonians who had married any of the Asiatic women should be registered. They were over 10,000 in number; and to these Alexander made presents on account of their weddings.

5. He now thought it a favourable opportunity to liquidate the debts of all the soldiers who had incurred them; and for this purpose he ordered that a register should be made of how much each man owed, in order that they might receive the money. At first only a few registered their names, fearing that this had been instituted as a test by Alexander, to discover which of the soldiers found their pay insufficient for their expenses, and which of them were extravagant in their mode of living. When he was informed that most of them were not registering their names, but that those who had borrowed money on bonds were concealing the fact, he reproached them for their distrust of him. For he said that it was not right either that the king should deal otherwise than sincerely with his subjects, or that any of those ruled by him should think that he would deal otherwise than sincerely with them. Accordingly, he had tables placed in the camp with money upon them; and he appointed men to manage the distribution of it. He ordered the debts of all who showed a money-bond to be liquidated without the debtors' names being any longer registered. Consequently, the men believed that Alexander was dealing sincerely with them; and the fact that they were not known was a greater pleasure to them than the fact that they ceased to be in debt. This presentation to the army is said to have amounted to 20,000 talents. He also gave presents to particular individuals, according as each man was held in honour for his merit or valour, if he had become conspicuous in crises of danger. Those who were distinguished for their personal gallantry he crowned with

golden chaplets: first, Peucestas, the man who had held the shield over him; second, Leonnatus, who also had held his shield over him, and moreover had incurred dangers in India and won a victory in Ora. For he had posted himself with the forces left with him against the Oritians and the tribes living near them, who were trying to effect a revolution, and had conquered them in battle. He also seemed to have managed other affairs in Ora with great success. In addition to these, he crowned Nearchus for his successful voyage round the coast from the land of the Indians through the Great Sea;—for this officer had now arrived at Susa. Besides these three, he crowned Onesicritus, the pilot of the royal ship; as well as Hephaestion and the rest of the confidential body-guards.

6. The viceroys from the newly-built cities and the rest of the territory subdued in war came to him, bringing with them youths just growing into manhood to the number of 30,000, all of the same age, whom Alexander called Epigoni. They had been accoutred with Macedonian arms, and exercised in military discipline after the Macedonian system. The arrival of these is said to have vexed the Macedonians, who thought that Alexander was contriving every means in his power to free himself from future need of their services. For the same reason also the sight of his Median dress was no small cause of dissatisfaction to them; and the weddings celebrated in the Persian fashion were displeasing to most of; them, even including some of those who married, although they had been greatly honoured by their being put on the same level with the king in the marriage ceremony. They were offended at Peucestas, the satrap of Persist on account of his Persianizing both in dress and in speech, because the king was delighted by his adopting the Asiatic customs. They were disgusted that the Bactrian, Sogdianian, Arachotian, Zarangian, Arian, and Parthian horsemen, as well as the Persian horsemen called the Evacae, had been distributed among the squadrons of the Companion cavalry; as many of them at least as were seen to excel in reputation, fineness of stature, or any other good quality; and that a fifth cavalry division was added to these troops, not composed entirely of foreigners; but the whole body of cavalry was increased in number, and men were picked from the foreigners and put into it. Cophen, son of Artabazus, Hydarnes and Artiboles, sons of Mazaeus, Sisines and Phradasmenes, sons of Phrataphernes, viceroy of Parthia and Hyrcania, Histanes, son of Oxyartes and brother of Alexander's wife, Roxane, as well as Autobares and his brother Mithrobaeus were picked out and enrolled among the foot-guard in addition to the Macedonian officers. Over these Hystaspes the Bactrian was placed as commander; and Macedonian spears were given to them instead of the barbarian javelins which had thongs attached to them. All this offended the Macedonians, who thought that Alexander was becoming altogether Asiatic in his ideas, and was holding the Macedonians themselves as well as their customs in a position of contempt …

8. When he arrived at Opis, he collected the Macedonians and announced that he intended to discharge from the army those who were useless for military service either from age or from being maimed in the limbs; and he said he would send them back to their own abodes. He also promised to give those who went back as much extra reward as would make them special objects of envy to those at home and arouse in the other Macedonians the wish to share similar dangers and labours. Alexander said this, no doubt, for the purpose of pleasing the Macedonians; but on the contrary they were, not without reason, offended by the speech which he delivered, thinking that now they were despised by him and deemed to be quite useless for military service. Indeed, throughout the whole of this expedition they had been offended at many other things; for his adoption of the Persian dress, thereby exhibiting his contempt for their opinion often caused them grief, as did also his accoutring the foreign soldiers called Epigoni in the Macedonian style, and the mixing of the alien horsemen among the ranks of the Companions. Therefore they could not remain silent and control themselves, but urged him to dismiss all of them from his army; and they advised him to prosecute the war in company with his father, deriding Amman by this remark. When Alexander heard this (for at that time he was more hasty in temper than heretofore, and no longer, as of old, indulgent to the Macedonians from having a retinue of foreign attendants), leaping down from the platform with his officers around him, he ordered the most conspicuous of the men who had tried to stir up the multitude to sedition to be arrested. He himself pointed out with his hand to the shield-bearing guards those whom they were to arrest, to the number of thirteen; and he ordered these to be led away to execution. When the rest, stricken with terror, became silent, he mounted the platform again, and spoke as follows:

9. "The speech which I am about to deliver will not be for the purpose of checking your start homeward, for, so far as I am concerned, you may depart wherever you wish; but for the purpose of making you understand when you take yourselves off, what kind of men you have been to us who have conferred such benefits upon you. In the first place, as is reasonable, I shall begin my speech from my father Philip. For he found you vagabonds and destitute of means, most of you clad in hides, feeding a few sheep up the mountain sides, for the protection of which you had to fight with small success against Illyrians, Triballians, and the border Thracians. Instead of the hides he gave you cloaks to wear, and from the mountains he led you down into the plains, and made you capable of fighting the neighbouring barbarians, so that you were no longer compelled to preserve yourselves by trusting rather to the inaccessible strongholds than to your own valour. He made you colonists of cities, which he adorned with useful laws and customs; and from being slaves and subjects, he made you rulers over those very barbarians by whom you yourselves, as well as your property, were previously liable to be carried off or ravaged. He also added the

greater part of Thrace to Macedonia, and by seizing the most conveniently situated places on the sea-coast, he spread abundance over the land from commerce, and made the working of the mines a secure employment. He made you rulers over the Thessalians, of whom you had formerly been in mortal fear; and by humbling the nation of the Phocians, he rendered the avenue into Greece broad and easy for you, instead of being narrow and difficult. The Athenians and Thebans, who were always lying in wait to attack Macedonia, he humbled to such a degree, I also then rendering him my personal aid in the campaign, that instead of paying tribute to the former and being vassals to the latter, those States in their turn procure security to themselves by our assistance. He penetrated into the Peloponnese, and after regulating its affairs, was publicly declared commander-in-chief of all the rest of Greece in the expedition against the Persian, adding this glory not more to himself than to the commonwealth of the Macedonians. These were the advantages which accrued to you from my father Philip; great indeed if looked at by themselves, but small if compared with those you have obtained from me. For though I inherited from my father only a few gold and silver goblets, and there were not even sixty talents in the treasury, and though I found myself charged with a debt of 500 talents owing by Philip, and I was obliged myself to borrow 800 talents in addition to these, I started from the country which could not decently support you, and forthwith laid open to you the passage of the Hellespont, though at that time the Persians held the sovereignty of the sea. Having overpowered the satraps of Darius with my cavalry, I added to your empire the whole of Ionia, the whole of Aeolis, both Phrygias and Lydia, and I took Miletus by siege. All the other places I gained by voluntary surrender, and I granted you the privilege of appropriating the wealth found in them. The riches of Egypt and Cyrene, which I acquired without fighting a battle, have come to you. Coele-Syria, Palestine, and Mesopotamia are your property. Babylon, Bactra, and Susa are yours. The wealth of the Lydians, the treasures of the Persians, and the riches of the Indians are yours; and so is the External Sea. You are viceroys, you are generals, you are captains. What then have I reserved to myself after all these labours, except this purple robe and this diadem? I have appropriated nothing myself, nor can any one point out my treasures, except these possessions of yours or the things which I am guarding on your behalf. Individually, however, I have no motive to guard them, since I feed on the same fare as you do, and I take only the same amount of sleep. Nay, I do not think that my fare is as good as that of those among you who live luxuriously; and I know that I often sit up at night to watch for you, that you may be able to sleep.

10. "But some one may say, that while you endured toil and fatigue, I have acquired these things as your leader without myself sharing the toil and fatigue. But who is there of you who knows that he has endured greater toil for me than I have for him? Come now, whoever of you has wounds, let him strip and show them, and I will

show mine in turn; for there is no part of my body, in front at any rate, remaining free from wounds; nor is there any kind of weapon used either for close combat or for hurling at the enemy, the traces of which I do not bear on my person. For I have been wounded with the sword in close fight, I have been shot with arrows, and I have been struck with missiles projected from engines of war; and though oftentimes I have been hit with stones and bolts of wood for the sake of your lives, your glory, and your wealth, I am still leading you as conquerors over all the land and sea, all rivers, mountains, and plains. I have celebrated your weddings with my own, and the children of many of you will be akin to my children. Moreover I have liquidated of all those who had incurred them, without inquiring too closely for what purpose they were contracted, though you received such high pay, and carry off so much booty whenever there is booty to be got after a siege. Most of you have golden crowns, the eternal memorials of your valour and of the honour you receive from me. Whoever has been killed has met with a glorious end and has been honoured with a splendid burial. Brazen statues of most of the slain have been erected at home, and their parents are held in honour) being released from all public service and from taxation. But no one of you has ever been killed in flight under my leadership. And now I was intending to send back those of you who are unfit for service, objects of envy to those at home; but since you all wish to depart, depart all of you! Go back and report at home that your king Alexander, the conqueror of the Persians, Medes, Bactrians, and Sacians; the man who has subjugated the Uxians, Arachotians, and Drangians; who has also acquired the rule of the Parthians, Chorasmians, and Hyrcanians, as far as the Caspian Sea; who has marched over the Caucasus, through the Caspian Gates; who has crossed the rivers Oxus and Tanais, and the Indus besides, which has never been crossed by any one else except Dionysus; who has also crossed the Hydaspes, Acesines, and Hydraotes, and who would have crossed the Hyphasis, if you had not shrunk back with alarm; who has penetrated into the Great Sea by both the mouths of the Indus; who has marched through the desert of Gadrosia, where no one ever before marched with an army; who on his route acquired possession of Carmania and the land of the Oritians, in addition to his other conquests, his Beet having in the meantime already sailed round the coast of the sea which extends from India to Persia—report that when you returned to Susa you deserted him and went away, handing him over to the protection of conquered foreigners. Perhaps this report of yours will be both glorious to you in the eyes of men and devout I ween in the eyes of the gods. Depart!"

PLUTARCH'S ACCOUNT OF THE ASSASSINATION OF JULIUS CAESAR

When Caesar entered, the senate stood up to show their respect to him, and of Brutus's confederates, some came about his chair and stood behind it, others met him, pretending to add their petitions to those of Tillius Cimber, in behalf of his brother, who was in exile; and they followed him with their joint supplications till he came to his seat. When he was sat down, he refused to comply with their requests, and upon their urging him further, began to reproach them severally for their importunities, when Tillius, laying hold of his robe with both his hands, pulled it down from his neck, which was the signal for the assault. Casca gave him the first cut, in the neck, which was not mortal nor dangerous, as coming from one who at the beginning of such a bold action was probably very much disturbed. Caesar immediately turned about, and laid his hand upon the dagger and kept hold of it. And both of them at the same time cried out, he that received the blow, in Latin, "Vile Casca, what does this mean?" and he that gave it, in Greek, to his brother, "Brother, help!" Upon this first onset, those who were not privy to the design were astonished and their horror and amazement at what they saw were so great, that they durst not fly nor assist Caesar, nor so much as speak a word. But those who came prepared for the business enclosed him on every side, with their naked daggers in their hands. Which way soever he turned, he met with blows, and saw their swords leveled at his face and eyes, and was encompassed, like a wild beast in the toils, on every side. For it had been agreed they should each of them make a thrust at him, and flesh themselves with his blood; for which reason Brutus also gave him one stab in the groin. Some say that he fought and resisted all the rest, shifting his body to avoid the blows, and calling out for

Plutarch, *Plutarch's Lives: Life of Marcus Brutus*, trans. John Dryden. Copyright in the Public Domain.

help, but that when he saw Brutus's sword drawn, he covered his face with his robe and submitted, letting himself fall, whether it were by chance, or that he was pushed in that direction by his murderers, at the foot of the pedestal on which Pompey's statue stood, and which was thus wetted with his blood. So that Pompey himself seemed to have presided, as it were, over the revenge done upon his adversary, who lay here at his feet, and breathed out his soul through his multitude of wounds, for they say he received three and twenty.

THE DEEDS OF THE DIVINE AUGUSTUS

INSCRIPTION OF AUGUSTUS (OCTAVIAN) WRITTEN 14 A.C.E.

TRANSLATED BY THOMAS BUSHNELL, BSG

1. In my nineteenth year, on my own initiative and at my own expense, I raised an army with which I set free the state, which was oppressed by the domination of a faction. For that reason, the senate enrolled me in its order by laudatory resolutions, when Gaius Pansa and Aulus Hirtius were consuls (43 B.C.E.), assigning me the place of a consul in the giving of opinions, and gave me the imperium. With me as propraetor, it ordered me, together with the consuls, to take care lest any detriment befall the state. But the people made me consul in the same year, when the consuls each perished in battle, and they made me a triumvir for the settling of the state.

2. I drove the men who slaughtered my father into exile with a legal order, punishing their crime, and afterwards, when they waged war on the state, I conquered them in two battles.

3. I often waged war, civil and foreign, on the earth and sea, in the whole wide world, and as victor I spared all the citizens who sought pardon. As for foreign nations, those which I was able to safely forgive, I preferred to preserve than to destroy. About five hundred thousand Roman citizens were sworn to me. I led something more than three hundred thousand of them into colonies and I returned them to their cities, after their stipend had been earned, and I assigned all of them fields or

gave them money for their military service. I captured six hundred ships in addition to those smaller than triremes.

4. Twice I triumphed with an ovation, and three times I enjoyed a curule triumph and twenty one times I was named emperor. When the senate decreed more triumphs for me, I sat out from all of them. I placed the laurel from the fasces in the Capitol, when the vows which I pronounced in each war had been fulfilled. On account of the things successfully done by me and through my officers, under my auspices, on earth and sea, the senate decreed fifty-five times that there be sacrifices to the immortal gods. Moreover there were 890 days on which the senate decreed there would be sacrifices. In my triumphs kings and nine children of kings were led before my chariot. I had been consul thirteen times, when I wrote this, and I was in the thirty-seventh year of tribunician power (14 A.C.E.).

5. When the dictatorship was offered to me, both in my presence and my absence, by the people and senate, when Marcus Marcellus and Lucius Arruntius were consuls (22 B.C.E.), I did not accept it. I did not evade the curatorship of grain in the height of the food shortage, which I so arranged that within a few days I freed the entire city from the present fear and danger by my own expense and administration. When the annual and perpetual consulate was then again offered to me, I did not accept it.

9. The senate decreed that vows be undertaken for my health by the consuls and priests every fifth year. In fulfillment of these vows they often celebrated games for my life; several times the four highest colleges of priests, several times the consuls. Also both privately and as a city all the citizens unanimously and continuously prayed at all the shrines for my health.

10. By a senate decree my name was included in the Saliar Hymn, and it was sanctified by a law, both that I would be sacrosanct for ever, and that, as long as I would live, the tribunician power would be mine. I was unwilling to be high priest in the place of my living colleague; when the people offered me that priesthood which my father had, I refused it. And I received that priesthood, after several years, with the death of him who had occupied it since the opportunity of the civil disturbance, with a multitude flocking together out of all Italy to my election, so many as had never before been in Rome, when Publius Sulpicius and Gaius Valgius were consuls (12 B.C.E.).

11. The senate consecrated the altar of Fortune the Bringer-back before the temples of Honor and Virtue at the Campanian gate for my return, on which it ordered the priests and Vestal virgins to offer yearly sacrifices on the day when I had returned to the city from Syria (when Quintus Lucretius and Marcus Vinicius were consuls (19 B.C.E.)), and it named that day Augustalia after my cognomen.

12. By the authority of the senate, a part of the praetors and tribunes of the plebs, with consul Quintus Lucretius and the leading men, was sent to meet me in Campania, which honor had been decreed for no one but me until that time. When I returned

to Rome from Spain and Gaul, having successfully accomplished matters in those provinces, when Tiberius Nero and Publius Quintilius were consuls (13 B.C.E.), the senate voted to consecrate the altar of August Peace in the field of Mars for my return, on which it ordered the magistrates and priests and Vestal virgins to offer annual sacrifices.

13. Our ancestors wanted Janus Quirinus to be closed when throughout the all the rule of the Roman people, by land and sea, peace had been secured through victory. Although before my birth it had been closed twice in all in recorded memory from the founding of the city, the senate voted three times in my principate that it be closed.

14. When my sons Gaius and Lucius Caesar, whom fortune stole from me as youths, were fourteen, the senate and Roman people made them consuls-designate on behalf of my honor, so that they would enter that magistracy after five years, and the senate decreed that on that day when they were led into the forum they would be included in public councils. Moreover the Roman knights together named each of them first of the youth and gave them shields and spears.

15. I paid to the Roman plebs, HS 300 per man from my father's will and in my own name gave HS 400 from the spoils of war when I was consul for the fifth time (29 B.C.E.); furthermore I again paid out a public gift of HS 400 per man, in my tenth consulate (24 B.C.E.), from my own patrimony; and, when consul for the eleventh time (23 B.C.E.), twelve doles of grain personally bought were measured out; and in my twelfth year of tribunician power (12–11 B.C.E.) I gave HS 400 per man for the third time. And these public gifts of mine never reached fewer than 250,000 men. In my eighteenth year of tribunician power, as consul for the twelfth time (5 B.C.E.), I gave to 320,000 plebs of the city HS 240 per man. And, when consul the fifth time (29 B.C.E.), I gave from my war-spoils to colonies of my soldiers each HS 1000 per man; about 120,000 men in the colonies received this triumphal public gift. Consul for the thirteenth time (2 B.C.E.), I gave HS 240 to the plebs who then received the public grain; they were a few more than 200,000.

16. I paid the towns money for the fields which I had assigned to soldiers in my fourth consulate (30 B.C.E.) and then when Marcus Crassus and Gnaeus Lentulus Augur were consuls (14 B.C.E.); the sum was about HS 600,000,000 which I paid out for Italian estates, and about HS 260,000,000 which I paid for provincial fields. I was first and alone who did this among all who founded military colonies in Italy or the provinces according to the memory of my age. And afterwards, when Tiberius Nero and Gnaeus Piso were consuls (7 B.C.E.), and likewise when Gaius Antistius and Decius Laelius were consuls (6 B.C.E.), and when Gaius Calvisius and Lucius Passienus were consuls (4 B.C.E.), and when Lucius Lentulus and Marcus Messalla were consuls (3 B.C.E.), and when Lucius Caninius and Quintus Fabricius were consuls (2 B.C.E.), I paid out rewards in cash to the soldiers whom I had led into

their towns when their service was completed, and in this venture I spent about HS 400,000,000.

21. I built the temple of Mars Ultor on private ground and the forum of Augustus from war-spoils. I build the theater at the temple of Apollo on ground largely bought from private owners, under the name of Marcus Marcellus my son-in-law. I consecrated gifts from war-spoils in the Capitol and in the temple of divine Julius, in the temple of Apollo, in the tempe of Vesta, and in the temple of Mars Ultor, which cost me about HS 100,000,000. I sent back gold crowns weighing 35,000 to the towns and colonies of Italy, which had been contributed for my triumphs, and later, however many times I was named emperor, I refused gold crowns from the towns and colonies which they equally kindly decreed, and before they had decreed them.

22. Three times I gave shows of gladiators under my name and five times under the name of my sons and grandsons; in these shows about 10,000 men fought. Twice I furnished under my name spectacles of athletes gathered from everywhere, and three times under my grandson's name. I celebrated games under my name four times, and furthermore in the place of other magistrates twenty-three times. As master of the college I celebrated the secular games for the college of the Fifteen, with my colleague Marcus Agrippa, when Gaius Furnius and Gaius Silanus were consuls (17 B.C.E.). Consul for the thirteenth time (2 B.C.E.), I celebrated the first games of Mas, which after that time thereafter in following years, by a senate decree and a law, the consuls were to celebrate. Twenty-six times, under my name or that of my sons and grandsons, I gave the people hunts of African beasts in the circus, in the open, or in the amphitheater; in them about 3,500 beasts were killed.

26. I extended the borders of all the provinces of the Roman people which neighbored nations not subject to our rule. I restored peace to the provinces of Gaul and Spain, likewise Germany, which includes the ocean from Cadiz to the mouth of the river Elbe. I brought peace to the Alps from the region which i near the Adriatic Sea to the Tuscan, with no unjust war waged against any nation. I sailed my ships on the ocean from the mouth of the Rhine to the east region up to the borders of the Cimbri, where no Roman had gone before that time by land or sea, and the Cimbri and the Charydes and the Semnones and the other Germans of the same territory sought by envoys the friendship of me and of the Roman people. By my order and auspices two armies were led at about the same time into Ethiopia and into that part of Arabia which is called Happy, and the troops of each nation of enemies were slaughtered in battle and many towns captured. They penetrated into Ethiopia all the way to the town Nabata, which is near to Meroe; and into Arabia all the way to the border of the Sabaei, advancing to the town Mariba.

27. I added Egypt to the rule of the Roman people. When Artaxes, king of Greater Armenia, was killed, though I could have made it a province, I preferred, by the example of our elders, to hand over that kingdomto Tigranes, son of king Artavasdes,

and grandson of King Tigranes, through Tiberius Nero, who was then my step-son. And the same nation, after revolting and rebelling, and subdued through my son Gaius, I handed over to be ruled by King Ariobarzanes son of Artabazus, King of the Medes, and after his death, to his son Artavasdes; and when he was killed, I sent Tigranes, who came from the royal clan of the Armenians, into that rule. I recovered all the provinces which lie across the Adriatic to the east and Cyrene, with kings now possessing them in large part, and Sicily and Sardina, which had been occupied earlier in the slave war.

28. I founded colonies of soldiers in Africa, Sicily, Macedonia, each Spain, Greece, Asia, Syria, Narbonian Gaul, and Pisidia, and furthermore had twenty-eight colonies founded in Italy under my authority, which were very populous and crowded while I lived.

32. To me were sent supplications by kings: of the Parthians, Tiridates and later Phrates son of king Phrates, of the Medes, Artavasdes, of the Adiabeni, Artaxares, of the Britons, Dumnobellaunus and Tincommius, of the Sugambri, Maelo, of the Marcomanian Suebi (…) (-)rus. King Phrates of the Parthians, son of Orodes, sent all his sons and grandsons into Italy to me, though defeated in no war, but seeking our friendship through the pledges of his children. And in my Principate many other peoples experienced the faith of the Roman people, of whom nothing had previously existed of embassies or interchange of friendship with the Roman people.

33. The nations of the Parthians and Medes received from me the first kings of those nations which they sought by emissaries: the Parthians, Vonones son of king Phrates, grandson of king Orodes, the Medes, Ariobarzanes, son of king Artavasdes, grandson of king Aiobarzanes.

34. In my sixth and seventh consulates (28–27 B.C.E.), after putting out the civil war, having obtained all things by universal consent, I handed over the state from my power to the dominion of the senate and Roman people. And for this merit of mine, by a senate decree, I was called Augustus and the doors of my temple were publicly clothed with laurel and a civic crown was fixed over my door and a gold shield placed in the Julian senate-house, and the inscription of that shield testified to the virtue, mercy, justice, and piety, for which the senate and Roman people gave it to me. After that time, I exceeded all in influence, but I had no greater power than the others who were colleagues with me in each magistracy.

35. When I administered my thirteenth consulate (2 B.C.E.), the senate and Equestrian order and Roman people all called me father of the country, and voted that the same be inscribed in the vestibule of my temple, in the Julian senate-house, and in the forum of Augustus under the chariot which had been placed there for me by a decision of the senate. When I wrote this I was seventy-six years old.

JUVENAL

THE EMANCIPATED WOMEN OF THE EARLY ROMAN EMPIRE

Yet a musical wife is not so bad as some presumptuous flat-chest busybody who rushes around the town, gate-crashing all-male meetings, talking back straight faced to an uniformed General and in her husband's presence.

She knows all the news of the world, what's cooking in Thrace or in China, just what the stepmother did with her stepson behind closed doors, who has fallen in love, which gallant is all the rage. She will tell you who got the widow pregnant, and in which month … She is on the latest gossip and rumors as soon as they reach the city gates, or invents her own, information …

Does she visit the baths: only then are her oil jars and the rest of her clobber transferred their. First she works out with the weights and dumb-bells. Then, when her arms are aching, the masseur takes over, craftily slipping one hand along her thigh, and … Lastly she makes for the sear-room. She loves to sit there amid all the hubbub, perspiring. Meanwhile at home her unfortunate guests are nearly dead with hunger.

Juvenal, *Juvenal and Persius* (The Loeb Classical Library), trans. G. G. Ramsay. Copyright in the Public Domain.

MAINCHAEAN HYMNS
(CENTRAL ASIA 200–700 CE)

I. HYMN ON THE THIRD MESSENGER AND THE ARCHONS (PARTHIAN)

He (the Third Messenger) takes the Light away from them (the demons) in many forms and fashions, by gentle means and harsh. He releases the captives from bondage. He purifies His own life and he exhorts them (Archons) to approach the visible form and to follow its appearance. Bright *Sadves* (Maiden of Light) show her form to the Demon of Wrath. She seduces him with her own appearance, and he things it is real. He sows his seed (he lets his seed fall), ... he groans when he no longer sees her form. Light is born in the sphere of the world; she passes it on to the higher powers. Filth and dross flow from him to the earth. They clothe themselves in manifold forms and are reborn in many fruits. The dark Demon of Wrath is ashamed, for in his confusion he had become naked. He had not attained the heights, and he had been robbed of whatever he had achieved.

II. HYMN ABOUT THE CAPTIVITY OF LIGHT (PARTHIAN)

Lo, that great Kingdom of Salvation waits on high, Ready for those who have *gnosis,* so that they may finally find peace there. Sinful, dark *Pesus* (mother of the first couple) runs hither and thither brutishly, She gives no peace at all to the upper and the lower limbs of

Light, She seizes and binds the Light in the six great bodies, In earth, water and fire, wind, plants and animals. She fashions it into many forms; she molds it into many figures; She fetters it in a prison so that it may not ascend to the height She weaves a net around it on all sides, she piles it up; she sets a watchman over it. Greed and lust are made it fellow-captives. She mixes destructive air into those six great bodies. She nurtures her own body but destroys their sons. The powers of Light on high confuse all the demons of wrath, The son of that *Pesus,* who is in a higher place.

III. COSMOGONICAL HYMN

That king of the demons (dewan) was moved towards the Light by envy … He wished to seize this mighty warlike one (the First Man). God, the highest of the gods, *Zurvan* was convulsed in battle with darkness, poison and burning. *Az,* the Demoness of Greed, that evil mother of all demons grew angry, and she stirred up great turmoil to aid her own soul. And from the impurity of the demons and from the filth of the she-demons she fashioned the body and entered into it herself … She (*Az*) made him (the first person) as though blind and deaf, senseless and confused, so that he might not know his origin and his family (the Realm of Light). She created the body as the prison … she filled it with hate and sin, anger and vengeance. Then *Ohrmzid,* the Lord, had mercy upon the souls and he descended to the earth in the form of man (Jesus or Third Messenger). He put to shame the evil *Az,* he made visible to Adam and clearly showed him all that had been and that was to be. In a flash he revealed to him that *Ohrmizd,* the Lord, had not himself created this fleshly body and had not imprisoned the soul. Resurrection was the destiny of the discerning soul of that fortunate one (Adam). He believed in the message of Ohrmizd, the good Lord. He eagerly accepted all the commandments, ordinances and seals of virtue, like a mighty hero, he put off the mortal body and was redeemed eternally. He was lifted up to Paradise, to the Realm of the Blessed.

IV. THE SECOND COMING OF JESUS (PERSIAN WITH PARTHIAN WORDS)

Speak to me, Lord and Friends, and reveal to me, Son of the Most Beloved (Jesus), the time of your coming, when you will appear at the end. Oh great Redeemer, my Teacher, speak of that time and its signs. The speakers, the righteous and chosen ones, who must live in the Realm of the Lie, Do not accumulate herds and belongings. Therefore they are persecuted. How long will the poor and the Family of Peace be persecuted? … You of compassionate races, tell of the coming subjugation of the sinners that are now exalted. The strong and valiant Son of the Most Beloved taught me what I had asked him: The time, the coming years and periods, will be different (from now), because of the ensuing battles. For the years shall flow like water in the rivers. Now that time is near at hand. That heretic that now rejoice shall you then vanquish, you Wrathful One. They will be persecuted, as they have persecuted. Then shall those who have wept be joyful, and those who now laugh weep. The righteous religion (den) shall hold sway over false teachings and nations. Persecution and suppression shall then be recompenses by eternal life.

V. THE TRIUMPH OF LIGHT

They will be joined together, the limbs (dispersed particles of Light), to the new Aeon, the Land of Greatness. The New Paradise and the eternal Realm of Light will be united into one, like a single rock and a single body, eternally, securely and forever. The demon of Darkness will be buried together with his abyss within that new and noble building. They will make the New Paradise just like that eternal Land of Light with divine streams springing and sweet winds blowing through it For the nature (redeemed Light) … they will prepare thrones, and they will … in the new Aeons. They will make and establish many splendid thrones for the Last Prince (Last God [a giant]), together with all the Fathers, the prosperous gods. All the beings of Light, the righteous Elect and the Hearers, who have endured much suffering, will rejoice with the Father (The First Man; Lord of Paradise). They will be glad and rejoice, and they will reign over His foes and the rebels in the New Aeon. For they have fought together with Him (First Man), and they have overcome and vanquished the Dark One who had boasted in vain.

Third Messenger: Jesus First Man: Adam

THE GOSPEL OF THOMAS
COPTIC EGYPTIAN
2ND–3RD CE

These are the secret words which the living Jesus spoke, and Didymus Judas Thomas wrote them down.

(1) And he said: He who shall find the interpretation of the words shall not taste of death.

(2) Jesus said: He who seeks, let him not cease seeking until: finds; and when he finds he will be troubled, and if he is troubled, he will be amazed, and he will reign over the All.

(3) Jesus said: If those who lead you say unto you: Behold, the Kingdom is in heaven, then the birds of the heaven will be before you. If they say unto you: It is in the sea, then the fish will be before you. But the Kingdom is within you, and it is outside of you. When you know yourselves, then shall you be known, and you shall know that you are the sons of the living Father. But if ye do not know yourselves, then you are in poverty, and you are poverty.

(4) Jesus said: The man aged in his days will not hesitate ask a little child of seven days about the place of life, and he shall live. For there are many first who shall be last, and they shall become a single one.

(5) Jesus said: Know what is before thy face, and what hidden from thee shall be revealed unto thee; for there is nothing hidden which shall not be made manifest.

(6) His disciples asked him and said unto him: Wilt thou that we fast? And how shall we pray? Shall we give alms? And what rules shall we observe in eating? Jesus said:

Do not lie; and that which you hate, do not do. For all things are revealed before heaven. For there is nothing hidden which shall not be manifest, and there is nothing covered which shall remain without being uncovered.

(7) Jesus said: Blessed is the lion which the man shall eat, and the lion become man; and cursed is the man whom the lion shall eat, and the lion become man.

(8) And he said: Man is like a wise fisherman, who cast his net into the sea and drew it up from the sea full of small fish. Among them the wise fisherman found a large good fish. He threw down all the small fish into the sea; he chose the large fish without trouble. He that hath ears to hear, let him hear.

(9) Jesus said: Behold, the sower went forth, he filled his hand, he cast. Some fell upon the road; the birds came and gathered them. Others fell on the rock, and sent no root down to the earth nor did they sprout any ear up to heaven. And others fell on the thorns; they choked the seed, and the worm ate them. And others fell on the good earth, and brought forth good fruit unto heaven, some sixty-fold and some an hundred and twenty-fold.

(10) Jesus said: I have cast fire upon the world, and behold I guard it until it is ablaze.

THE GOSPEL ACCORDING TO MARY

5TH CENTURY PAPYRUS GREEK TEXT

Peter said to Mary, 'Sister, we know that the Savior loved you more than other women [cf. John 11:5, Luke 10:38–42]. Tell us the words of the Savior which you have in mind since you know them; and we do not, nor have we heard of them."

Mary answered and said, "What is hidden from you I will impart to you." And she began to say the following words to them. "I," she said, "I saw the Lord in a vision and I said to him, "Lord, I saw you today in a vision." He answered and said to me, "Blessed are you, since you did not waver at the sight of me. For where the mind is, there is your countenance" [cf. Matt. 6:21]. I said to him, "Lord, the mind which sees the vision, does it see it through the soul or through the spirit?" The Savior answered and said, "It sees neither through the soul nor through the spirit, but the mind, which is between the two, which sees the vision, and it is …'"

"… and Desire said, "I did not see you descend; but now I see you rising. Why do you speak falsely, when you belong to me?" The soul answered and said, "I saw you, but you did not see me or recognize me; I served you as a garment and you did not recognize me." After it had said this, it went joyfully and gladly away. Again it came to the third power, Ignorance. This power questioned the soul: "Whither are you going? You were bound in wickedness, you were bound indeed. Judge not" [cf. Matt. 7:1]. And the soul said, "Why do you judge me, when I judged not? I was bound, though I did not bind. I was not recognized, but I recognized that all will go free, things both earthly and heavenly." After the soul had left the third power behind, it rose upward, and saw the fourth power, which had seven forms. The first form is darkness, the second desire, the third ignorance, the fourth the arousing of death, the fifth is the kingdom of the flesh, the sixth is the wisdom of the folly of the flesh, the seventh is wrathful wisdom. These are the seven participants in wrath. They ask the soul, "Whence do you come, killer of men, or where are you going, conqueror of space?" The soul answered and said, "What seizes me is killed; what turns me about is overcome; my desire has come to an end and ignorance is dead. In a world I was saved from a world, and in a "type," from a higher "type" and from the fetter of the impotence of knowledge, the existence of which is temporal. From this time I will reach rest in the time of the moment of the Aeon in silence.'"

When Mary had said this, she was silent, since the Savior had spoken thus far with her. But Andrew answered and said to the brethren, "Say what you think concerning what she said. For I do not believe that the Savior said this. For certainly these teachings are of other ideas."

Peter also opposed her in regard to these matters and asked them about the Savior. "Did he then speak secretly with a woman [cf. John 4:27], in preference to us, and not openly?

Are we to turn back and all listen to her? Did he prefer her to us?" Then Mary grieved and said to Peter, "My brother Peter, what do you think? Do you think that I thought this up myself in my heart or that I am lying concerning the Savior?"

Levi answered and said to Peter, "Peter, you are always irate. Now I see that you are contending against the woman like the adversaries. But if the Savior made her worthy, who are you to reject her? Surely the Savior knew her very well [cf. Luke 10:38–42]. For this reason he loved her more than us [cf. John 11:5]. And we should rather be ashamed and put on the Perfect Man, to form us [?] as he commanded us, and proclaim the gospel, without publishing a further commandment or a further law than the one which the Savior spoke." When Levi had said this, they began to go out in order to proclaim him and preach him.

QUR'AN
SURA 99 AND 30

SURA 99: EARTHQUAKES

When the earth is shaken to her (utmost) convulsion,

And the earth throws up her burdens (from within),

And man cries (distressed): "What is the matter with her?"—

On that Day will she declare her tidings:

For that thy Lord will have given her inspiration.

On that Day will men proceed in companies sorted out, to be shown the deeds that they

(had done).

Then shall anyone who has done an atom's weight of good, see it!

And anyone who has done an atom's weight of evil, shall see it.

SURA 30: ROMANS/BYZANTINES

A. L. M.

The Roman Empire has been defeated—

In a land close by; but they, (even) after (this) defeat of theirs, will soon be victorious—-

Within a few years. With Allah is the Decision, in the past and in the Future: on that Day

Qur'an, trans. Alexander Ross. Copyright in the Public Domain.

shall the Believers rejoice—

With the help of Allah. He helps whom He will, and He is exalted in might, most merciful.

(It is) the promise of Allah. Never does Allah depart from His promise: but most men understand not.

They know but the outer (things) in the life of this world: but of the End of things they are heedless.

Do they not reflect in their own minds? Not but for just ends and for a term appointed, did Allah create the heavens and the earth, and all between them: yet are there truly many

among men who deny the meeting with their Lord (at the Resurrection)!

Do they not travel through the earth, and see what was the end of those before them? They were superior to them in strength: they tilled the soil and populated it in greater numbers than these have done: there came to them their messengers with Clear (Signs).

(Which they rejected, to their own destruction): It was not Allah Who wronged them, but

they wronged their own souls.

In the long run evil in the extreme will be the End of those who do evil; for that they rejected the Signs of Allah, and held them up to ridicule.

It is Allah Who begins (the process of) creation; then repeats it; then shall ye be brought back to Him.

On the Day that the Hour will be established, the guilty will be struck dumb with despair.

No intercessor will they have among their "Partners" and they will (themselves) reject their "Partners."

On the Day that the Hour will be established,—that Day shall (all men) be sorted out. Then those who have believed and worked righteous deeds, shall be made happy in a Mead of Delight.

And those who have rejected Faith and falsely denied our Signs and the meeting of the Hereafter,—such shall be brought forth to Punishment.

So (give) glory to Allah, when ye reach eventide and when ye rise in the morning;

Yea, to Him be praise, in the heavens and on earth; and in the late afternoon and when the

day begins to decline.

It is He Who brings out the living from the dead, and brings out the dead from the living,

and Who gives life to the earth after it is dead: and thus shall ye be brought out (from the

dead).

Among His Signs in this, that He created you from dust; and then,—behold, ye are men

scattered (far and wide)!

And among His Signs is this, that He created for you mates from among yourselves, that

ye may dwell in tranquillity with them, and He has put love and mercy between your (hearts): verily in that are Signs for those who reflect.

And among His Signs is the creation of the heavens and the earth, and the variations in your languages and your colors: verily in that are Signs for those who know.

And among His Signs is the sleep that ye take by night and by day, and the quest that ye (make for livelihood) out of His Bounty: verily in that are signs for those who hearken.

And among His Signs, He shows you the lightning, by way both of fear and of hope, and

He sends down rain from the sky and with it gives life to the earth after it is dead: verily in that are Signs for those who are wise.

And among His Signs is this, that heaven and earth stand by His Command: then when

He calls you, by a single call, from the earth, behold, ye (straightway) come forth.

AL-KWARIZMI
(780–850 CE)
ON ALGEBRA

al-Kitab al-mukhtasar fi hisab al-jabr w'al-muqabala or The Compendious Book on Calculation by Completion or Restoring and Balancing.

If the instance be, "ten and thing to be multiplied by thing less ten," then this is the same as "if it were said thing and ten by thing less ten. You say, therefore, thing multiplied by thing is a square positive; and ten by thing is ten things positive; and minus ten by thing is ten things negative. You now remove the positive by the negative, then there only remains a square. Minus ten multiplied by ten is a hundred, to be subtracted from the square. This, therefore, altogether, is a square less a hundred dirhams."

Abū 'Abdallāh Muhammad ibn Mūsā al-Khwārizmī, *The Compendious Book on Calculation by Completion and Balancing*, trans. F. Rosen. Copyright in the Public Domain.

THE STORY OF HUSAYN'S DEATH
SHI'ITE MUSLIM TRADITION
BATTLE OF KARBALA 680 CE

Then Husayn (Son of Ali, grandson of Prophet Muhammad) advanced toward the crowds and raising his sword and despaired of life and called the people for a combat, and he killed everyone that met him, until he killed so many of them. Then he attacked the right wing and said:

> To be killed is better than being ashamed
> and the shame is better than going to hell
> by Allah this and that are not my companions

Then he attacked the left wing and said:

> I am Husayn ben 'Ali
> I've sworn not to bend
> I shall protect the children of my father
> and go on with the way of the prophet

… when Shimr saw that, he ordered the knights to be at the back of the foot soldiers and then ordered the archers to shoot at him and so they did until his shield became like a hedgehog, and then Shimr came with some fellows and blocked the way between him and his harem (Husayn's wives and children). Then Husayn shouted: woe to you! O followers of Abu-Sufyan, if you have no religion and were not afraid of the judgment day then be

The Battle of Karbala, trans. Taher Al-Shemaly. Copyright in the Public Domain.

free in this life and turn back to your ancestries if you were Arabs as you claim, then Shimr called him and said: what are you saying O son of Fatima?

Then he replied: I say, I am fighting you and you are fighting me and the women have no guilt, so turn away your ignorant people and your tyrants and don't let them attack my harem as long I am alive. Then Shimr said: you've got that O son of Fatima, and then he shouted: stay away from the harem of the man and point at him directly, by my life he is a graceful man!

… Then he (Husayn) got back to fight the enemies of Allah and remained in the fight until he was injured with 72 injuries. Then he stood to take a rest and he was weak to continue fighting, and while he was standing, Abul-Hotoof Al-Jo'fi threw a stone at him, and some say with an arrow, and it hit his forehead, so he took a cloth to clean the blood from his forehead, and while doing so a poisoned arrow with three heads arrived into his heart! Then he (Husayn) said: by the name of Allah and by Allah, and on the way of the prophet of Allah, then he raised his head to the sky and said: O my Lord, verily You know that they are killing a man that has no likings on earth, and then he took the arrow and got him out from his back and the blood gushed out like the rain! The blood gushing made him exhausted so he sat on the ground and turning his neck around, and in that situation, Málik ben Al-Nisr Al-Kindi came to him and cursed him and hit his honorable head with the sword, and there was a cloak over his head, and the cloak got filled with blood, and Husayn: may you never eat with your hand neither drink, and may Allah gather you with the wrong people, and then he threw the cloak away and put his hood …

Then Husayn remained on the ground for some time although they could have killed him, but every tribe was depending on the other and hated to do so. Hilál ben Náfi' said: I was standing with the fellows of 'Umar ben Sa'd when a caller shouted: O be happy prince, this is Shimr killed Husayn, so I went out between the two rows and took a look at him and I've seen him protecting himself, and by Allah, I've never seen a man that got dipped in his blood that would be better than him, and no one with a face brighter than his, and I was busy looking at the halo of his face and the beauty of his shape and didn't think of killing him, and while he was in that situation he asked for water, and I heard a man saying: by Allah you shall not drink the water until you go to hell and drink from its fire, and I heard him reply: I shall go to hell and drink of its fire? No by Allah, I shall go to my grandfather the prophet of Allah (PUH) and shall live with him in his own home in a firmly established in the favor of a Mighty King, and I shall drink a water that is not dirty and I shall complain to him about you've done to me, and all of them got angry like if Allah never planted anything of mercy in their hearts. Then Al-Husayn (PUH) raised his hand to the sky and said: Allah, O You of the High Place, of the Mighty Power, of the Great Wisdom, not in need of the creatures, and high in His Pride, verily You are Able for whatever You desire, close in mercy, and true with the promise, and Graceful with His favors, and a Tester of goodness, close whenever You are called, and surrounding whatever You have created, and verily You accept the repenting for those who repent, and verily

You are Able for what You desire, and verily You get whatever You want, Thankful if You have been praised, and You mention those who mention You, and I pray to You for my need, and ask You for my necessity, and go toward You when I am afraid and cry for my adversities, and I seek help from You when I am weak, and I depend on You when I am satisfied, Allah, judge between us and between those people for they have tricked us and let us down and betrayed us and killed us, and we are the Household of Your prophet, and the children of Your beloved Mohamad (Prophet of Islam) have chosen him for the Message, and made him to receive the inspirations, so make for us, O Lord, a relief from our matter O You the most Merciful of all. Patience over what You have destined O Lord, no other god but You, O Helper of those who need the help.

Then Shimr shouted at the knights and the foot soldiers: woe to you! what do you wait from the man? Kill him may your mothers be bereaved, and so they attacked him from all the sides and Zor'ah ben Shorayk hit him on his left shoulder, and Husayn hit Zor'ah and killed him. Then another man hit him on his holy shoulder with his sword and made him fall on his face, and he was sitting. Then he started to stand up and fall down, and then Sinán ben Anas Al-Nakh'ee stabbed him in his throat and took the spear out and stabbed him in his chest, and threw him with an arrow into his neck, so he then fell down and sat on the ground and took the arrow out from his neck and started to collect the blood with his hands and whenever they were full he would paint his head and his beard with it while saying: this is how shall I meet Allah, painted with blood and my rights have been taken.

Then 'Umar ben Sa'd said to Sinán ben Anas: get down woe to you! go to Husayn and make him rest, and then Sinán said to Khiwallá ben Yazeed: go and behead him, and Khiwallá went to do so but he got weakened and shocked, so Sinán said to him and some say Shimr said to him: may Allah disolve you arms, why are you shaking? Then Sinán got down and some say it was Shimr and he killed him and amputated his holy head while saying: I behead you and I know you are the master and the son of the prophet of Allah and the best of people from mother's and father's side, and then he gave the head to

Khiwallá and said to him: take it to the prince 'Umar ben Sa'd.

Then the crowds came to steal whatever he (PUH) had, thus his shirt was taken by Is-háq ben Khawiyyah Al-Hadhrami, and his pants were taken by Bahr ben Ka'b and his turban was taken by Al-Akhnas, and his shield was taken by 'Umar ben Sa'd, and his clothes were taken by a brother of Is-háq ben Khawiyyah, and his velvet was taken by Qays ben Al-Ash'ath ben Qays, and his cloak was taken by Málik ben Nisr, and his sword was taken by Al-Faláfis Al-Nahshali from the tribe of Dárim, and his sandals were taken by Al-Aswad ben Khálid, and his ring was taken by Bajdal ben Saleem Al-Kalbi who amputated the finger with the ring.

Muslim View of the Crusaders and Europeans

Usamah ibn Munqidh
(11th–12th CE)

A case illustrating their curious medicine is the following:

The lord of al-Munaytirah (in Lebanon) wrote to my uncle asking him to dispatch a physician to treat certain sick persons among his people. They brought before me a knight in whose leg an abscess had grown, and a woman afflicted with imbecility. To the knight I applied a small medicine until the abscess opened and became well; and the woman I put on diet and made her humor wet. Then a Frankish physician came to them and said: "This man knows nothing about treating them." He then said to the knight: "Which wouldst thou prefer, living with one leg or dying with two?" The latter replied, "Living with one leg." The physician said: "Bring me a strong knight and a sharp ax." A knight came with the ax. And I was standing by. Then the physician laid the leg on the patient on the block of wood and bade the knight strike his leg with the ax and chopped it off at one blow … but the leg was not severed. He dealt another blow, upon which the marrow of the leg flowed out and the patient died on the spot. He then examined the woman and said: "this is a woman in whose head there is a devil which has possessed her. Shave off her hair." He took a razor, made a deep cruciform incision on it, peeled off the skin at the middle of the incision until the bone of the skull was exposed and rubbed it with salt. The woman expired instantly. There up I asked them whether my services were needed any longer, and when they replied in the negative I returned home, having learned of their medicine what I knew not before.

Usāmah ibn-Munqidh, *An Arab-Syrian Gentleman and Warrior in the Period of the Crusades: Memoirs of Usāmah ibn-Munqidh*, trans. Philip K. Hitti. Copyright © 1929 by Columbia University Press. Reprinted with permission.

Diagnosis of Small-pox
Zakariya Razi (9th CE)
From the city of Ray (Tehran)

The eruption of smallpox is preceded by a continued fever, pain in the back, itching in the nose and nightmares during sleep. These are the more acute symptoms of its approach together with a noticeable pain in the back accompanied by fever and an itching felt by the patient all over his body. A swelling of the face appears, which comes and goes, and one notices an overall inflammatory color noticeable as a strong redness on both cheeks and around both eyes. One experiences a heaviness of the whole body and great restlessness, which expresses itself as a lot of stretching and yawning. There is a pain in the throat and chest and one finds it difficult to breath and cough. Additional symptoms are: dryness of breath, thick spittle, hoarseness of the voice, pain and heaviness of the head, restlessness, nausea and anxiety. (Note the difference: restlessness, nausea and anxiety occur more frequently with "measles" than with smallpox. At the other hand, pain in the back is more apparent with smallpox than with measles). Altogether one experiences heat over the whole body, one has an inflamed colon and one shows an overall shining redness, with a very pronounced redness of the gums."

MORE ON SMALL-POX:

"Smallpox appears when blood 'boils' and is infected, resulting in vapours being expelled. Thus juvenile blood (which looks like wet extracts appearing on the skin) is being transformed into richer blood, having the color of mature wine. At this stage, smallpox shows up essentially as 'bubbles found in wine'—(as blisters)—… this disease can also occur at other times—(meaning: not only during childhood). The best thing to do during this first stage is to keep away from it, otherwise this disease might turn into an epidemic."

Muhammad ibn Zakariyā Rāzī, *A Treatise on the Small-Pox and Measles*, trans. William Alexander Greenhill. Copyright in the Public Domain.

TACITUS

GERMANIA

The Kings in Germany owe their election to the nobility of their birth; the generals are chosen for their valor. The power of the former is not arbitrary or unlimited; the latter command more by warlike example than by their authority. To be of a prompt and daring spirit in battle, and to attack in the front of the lines, is the popular character of the chieftain: when admired for his braver, he is sure to be obeyed. Jurisdiction is vested in the priests. It is theirs to sit in judgment upon all offences. By them, delinquents are put in irons, and chastised with stripes. The power of punishing is in no other hands. When exerted by the priests, it has neither the air of vindictive justice, nor of military execution; it is rather a religious sentence, inflicted with the sanction of the god, who, according to the German creed, attends their armies on the day of battle. To impress on their minds the idea of a tutelary deity, they carry with them to the field certain images and banners, taken from their usual depository, the religious groves. A circumstance which greatly tends to inflame them with heroic ardor, is the manner in which their battalions are formed. They are neither mustered nor embodied by chance. They fight in clans, united by the next-of-kin, a family of warriors. In the heat of the engagement, the soldier hears the shrieks of his wife, and the cries of his children.

Marriage is considered as a strict and sacred institution. In the national character there is nothing so truly commendable. To be counted with one wife, is peculiar to the Germans. They differ, in their respect, from all other savage nations. There are a few instances of polygamy, not, however, the effect of loose desire, but occasioned by the ambition of various families, who court the alliance of the chief distinguished by the nobility of his rank and character. The bride brings no portion, she receives a dowry from her husband … The art of intriguing by clandestine letters is unknown to both sexes. Populous as the country is, adultery is rarely heard of: when detected the punishment is instant, and inflicted by the husband. He cuts off the hair of his guilty wife and having assembled her relations, expels her naked from his house, pursuing her with stripes through the village.

Their beverage is a liquor drawn from barley or from wheat, and, like the juice of the grape, fermented to a spirit. The settlers on the banks of the Rhine provide themselves with wine. Their food is of the simplest kinds; wild apples, the flesh of an animal recently killed, or cheese. Without skill in cookery, or without seasoning to stimulate the palate, they eat to satisfy nature. But they do not drink merely to quench their thirst. Indulge their love of liquor to the excess which they require and you need not employ the terror of your arms; their own vices will subdue them.

VIKING LIFE

AHMED IBN FADLAN
(10TH CE)

I saw how the Northmen had arrived with their wares, and pitched their camp beside the Volga. Never did I see people so gigantic; they are tall as palm trees, and florid and ruddy of complexion. They wear neither camisoles nor caftans, but the men among them wear a garment of rough cloth, which is thrown over one side, so that one hand remains free. Every one carries an axe, a dagger, and a sword, and without these weapons they are never seen. Their swords are broad, with wavy lines, and of Frankish make. From the tip of the fingernails to the neck, each man of them is tattooed with pictures of trees, living beings, and other things. The women carry, fastened to their breast, a little case of iron, coppers, silver, or gold, according to the wealth and resources of their husbands. Fastened to the case they wear a ring, and upon that a dagger, all attached to their breast. About their necks they wear gold and silver chains.

They are the filthiest race that God ever created. They do not wipe themselves after going to stool, nor wash themselves after a nocturnal pollution, any more than if they were wild asses … Each man has a couch, when he sits with the beautiful girls he has for sale. Here he is as likely as not to enjoy one of them while a friend looks on. At times several of them will be thus engaged at the same moment, each in full view of the others. Now and again a merchant will resort to a house to purchase a girl, and find her master thus embracing her, and not giving over until he has fully had his will.

If they catch thief or a robber, they lead him to a thick and lofty tree, fasten a strong rope round him, string him up and let him hang until he drops to pieces by the action of the wind and rain.

Ahmad ibn Fadlan, *Journal of English and Germanic Philology*, ed. A. S. Cook. Copyright in the Public Domain.

I was told that the least of what they do for their chiefs when they die, is to consume them with fire. First they laid him in his grave—over which a roof was erected—for the space of ten days, until they had completed the cutting and sewing of his clothes. In the case of a poor man, however, they merely build for him a boat, in which they place him, and consume it with fire. At the death of a rich man, they bring together his goods, and divided them into three parts. The first of these is for his family; the second is expended to the garments they make; and with the third they purchase strong drink, against the day when the girl resigns herself to death, and is burned with her master. To the use of wine they abandon themselves in mad fashion, drinking it day and night; and not seldom does on dies with the cup in his hand.

GIOVANNI BOCCACCIO
DECAMERON (14TH CE)

NOVEL X.

A libech turns hermit, and is taught by Rustico, a monk, how the Devil is put in hell. She is afterwards conveyed thence, and becomes the wife of Neerbale.

Dioneo, observing that the queen's story, which he had followed with the closest attention, was now ended, and that it only remained for him to speak, waited not to be bidden, but smilingly thus began:

Gracious ladies, perchance you have not yet heard how the Devil is put in hell; wherefore, without deviating far from the topic of which you have discoursed throughout the day, I will tell you how 'tis done; it may be the lesson will prove inspiring; besides which, you may learn therefrom that, albeit Love prefers the gay palace and the dainty chamber to the rude cabin, yet, for all that, he may at times manifest his might in wilds matted with forests, rugged with alps, and desolate with caverns: whereby it may be understood that all things are subject to his sway.

But—to come to my story—I say that in the city of Capsa (Gafsa, in Tunis) in Barbary there was once a very rich man, who with other children had a fair and dainty little daughter, Alibech by name. Now Alibech, not being a Christian, and hearing many Christians, that were in the city, speak much in praise of the Christian Faith and the service of God, did one day inquire of one of them after what fashion it were possible to serve God with as few impediments as might be, and was informed that they served God best who most completely renounced the world and its affairs; like those who had fixed their abode in the wilds of the Thebaid desert. Whereupon, actuated by no sober predilection, but by childish impulse, the girl, who was very simple and about fourteen years of age, said never a word more of the matter, but stole away on the morrow, and quite alone set out to walk to the Thebaid desert; and, by force of resolution, albeit with no small suffering, she after some days reached those wilds; where, espying a cabin a great way off, she hid her thither, and found a holy man by the door, who, marvelling to see her there, asked her what she came there to seek. She answered that, guided by the spirit of God, she was come thither, seeking, if haply she might serve Him, and also find some one that might teach her how he ought to be served.

Marking her youth and great beauty, the worthy man, fearing lest, if he suffered her to remain with him, he should be ensnared by the Devil, commended her good intention, set before her a frugal repast of roots of herbs, crab-apples and dates, with a little water to wash them down, and said to her: "My daughter, there is a holy man not far from here, who is much better able to teach thee that of which thou art in quest than I am; go to him, therefore;" and he showed her the way. But when she was come whither she was directed, she met with the same answer as before, and so, setting forth again, she came at length to the cell of a young hermit, a worthy man and very devout—his name Rustico—whom she interrogated as she had the others. Rustico, being minded to make severe trial of his constancy, did not send her away, as the others had done, but kept her with him in his cell, and when night came, made her a little bed of palm-leaves; whereon he bade her compose herself to sleep. Hardly had she done so before the solicitations of the flesh joined battle with the powers of Rustico's spirit, and he, finding himself left in the lurch by the latter, endured not many assaults before he beat a retreat, and surrendered at discretion: wherefore he bade adieu to holy meditation and prayer and discipline, and fell a musing on the youth and beauty of his companion, and also how he might so order his conversation with her, that without seeming to her to be a libertine he might yet compass that which he craved of her.

So, probing her by certain questions, he discovered that she was as yet entirely without cognizance of man, and as simple as she seemed: wherefore he excogitated a plan for bringing her to pleasure him under color of serving God. He began by giving her a long lecture on the great enmity that subsists between God and the Devil; after which he gave her to understand that, God having condemned the Devil to hell, to put him there was of all services the most acceptable to God. The girl asking him how it might be done, Rustico answered:—"Thou shalt know it in a trice; thou hast but to do that which thou seest me do." Then, having divested himself of his scanty clothing, he threw himself stark naked on his knees, as if he would pray; whereby he caused the girl, who followed his example, to confront him in the same posture. Whereupon Rustico, seeing her so fair, felt an accession of desire, and therewith came an insurgence of the flesh, which Alibech marking with surprise, said:—"Rustico, what is this, which I see thee have, that so protrudes, and which I have not?"

"Oh! my daughter," said Rustico, "tis the Devil of whom I have told thee: and, seest thou? he is now tormenting me most grievously, insomuch that I am scarce able to hold out." Then:—"Praise be to God," said the girl, "I see that I am in better case than thou, for no such Devil have I." "Sooth sayst thou," returned Rustico; "but instead of him thou hast somewhat else that I have not." "Oh!" said Alibech, "what may that be?" "Hell," answered Rustico: "and I tell thee, that 'tis my belief that God has sent thee hither for the salvation of my soul; seeing that, if this Devil shall continue to plague me thus, then, so thou wilt have compassion on me and permit me to put him in hell, thou wilt both afford me great and exceeding great solace, and render to God an exceeding most acceptable service, if, as thou sayst, thou art come into these parts for such a purpose."

In good faith the girl made answer: "As I have hell to match your Devil, be it, my father, as and when you will." Whereupon:—"Bless thee, my daughter," said Rustico, "go we then, and put him there, that he leave me henceforth in peace." Which said, he took the girl to one of the beds and taught her the posture in which she must lie in order to incarcerate this spirit accursed of God. The girl, having never before put any devil in hell, felt on this first occasion a twinge of pain: wherefore she said to Rustico: "Of a surety, my father, he must be a wicked fellow, this devil, and in very truth a foe to God; for there is sorrow even in hell—not to speak of other places—when he is put there." "Daughter," said Rustico, "twill not be always so." And for better assurance thereof they put him there six times before they quitted the bed; whereby they so thoroughly abased his pride that he was fain to be quiet.

However, the proud fit returning upon him from time to time, and the girl addressing herself always obediently to its reduction, it so befell that she began to find the game agreeable, and would say to Rustico: "Now see I plainly that 'twas true, what the worthy men said at Capsa, of the service of God being so delightful: indeed I cannot remember that in aught that ever I did I had so much pleasure, so much solace, as in putting the Devil in hell; for which cause I deem it insensate folly on the part of any one to have a care to aught else than the service of God." Wherefore many a time she would come to Rustico, and say to him: "My father, 'twas to serve God that I came hither, and not to pass my days in idleness: go we then, and put the Devil in hell." And while they did so, she would now and again say: "I know not, Rustico, why the Devil should escape from hell; were he but as ready to stay there as hell is to receive and retain him, he would never come out of it."

So, the girl thus frequently inviting and exhorting Rustico to the service of God, there came at length a time when she had so thoroughly lightened his doublet that he shivered when another would have sweated; wherefore he began to instruct her that the Devil was not to be corrected and put in hell, save when his head was exalted with pride; adding, "and we by God's grace have brought him to so sober a mind that he prays God he may be left in peace;" by which means he for a time kept the girl quiet. But when she saw that Rustico had no more occasion for her to put the Devil in hell, she said to him one day: "Rustico, if thy Devil is chastened and gives thee no more trouble, my hell, on the other hand, gives me no peace; wherefore, I with my hell have holpen thee to abase the pride of thy Devil, so thou wouldst do well to lend me the aid of thy Devil to allay the fervent heat of my hell." Rustico, whose diet was roots of herbs and water, was scarce able to respond to her demands: he told her that "twould require not a few devils to allay the heat of hell; but that he would do what might be in his power; and so now and again he satisfied her; but so seldom that 'twas as if he had tossed a bean into the jaws of a lion. Whereat the girl, being fain of more of the service of God than she had, did somewhat repine.

However, the case standing thus (deficiency of power against superfluity of desire) between Rustico's Devil and Alibech's hell, it chanced that a fire broke out in Capsa, whereby the house of Alibech's father was burned, and he and all his sons and the rest of his household perished; so that Alibech was left sole heiress of all his estate. And a young gallant, Neerbale by name, who by reckless munificence had wasted all his substance, having discovered that she was alive, addressed himself to the pursuit of her, and, having found her in time to prevent the confiscation of her father's estate as an escheat for failure of heirs, took her, much to Rustico's relief and against her own will, back to Capsa, and made her his wife, and shared with her her vast patrimony. But before he had lain with her, she was questioned by the ladies of the manner in which she had served God in the desert; whereto she answered, that she had been wont to serve Him by putting the Devil in hell, and that Neerbale had committed a great sin, when he took her out of such service. The ladies being curious to know how the Devil was put in hell, the girl satisfied them, partly by words, partly by signs. Whereat they laughed exorbitantly (and still laugh) and said to her:—"Be not down-hearted, daughter; 'tis done here too; Neerbale will know well how to serve God with you in that way." And so the story passing from mouth to mouth throughout the city, it came at last to be a common proverb, that the most acceptable service that can be rendered to God is to put the Devil in hell; which proverb, having traveled hither across the sea, is still current. Wherefore, young ladies, you that have need of the grace of God, see to it that you learn how to put the Devil in hell, because 'tis mightily pleasing to God, and of great solace to both the parties, and much good may thereby be engendered and ensue.

Medieval Codes of Chivalry

MEDIEVAL CODES OF CHIVALRY

Thou shalt believe all that the Church teaches, and shalt observe all its directions. Thou shalt defend the Church. Thou shalt respect all weaknesses, and shalt constitute thyself the defender of them.

Thou shalt love the country in the which thou wast born. Thou shalt not recoil before the enemy.

Thou shalt make war against the Infidel without cessation, and without mercy. Thou shalt perform scrupulously thy feudal duties, if they be not contrary to the laws of God.

Thou shalt never lie, and shalt remain faithful to thy pledged word. Thou shalt be generous, and give largesse to everyone.

Thou shalt be everywhere and always the champion of the Right and the Good against Injustice and Evil.

CHARLEMAGNE'S CODE OF CHIVALRY THE SONG OF ROLAND (11TH CE)

To fear God and maintain His Church
To serve the liege lord in valor and faith

Léon Gautier, *Chivalry*, trans. Henry Frith. Copyright in the Public Domain.
The Song of Roland, trans. Charles Kenneth Scott Moncrieff. Copyright in the Public Domain.

To protect the weak and defenseless
To give succor to widows and orphans
To refrain from the wanton giving of offence
To live by honor and for glory
To despise pecuniary reward
To fight for the welfare of all
To obey those placed in authority
To guard the honor of fellow knights
To eschew unfairness, meanness and deceit
To keep faith
At all times to speak the truth
To persevere to the end in any enterprise begun
To respect the honor of women
Never to refuse a challenge from an equal
Never to turn the back upon a foe.

RULES OF COURTLY LOVE
ANDREAS CAPELLANUS
(11TH CE)

I.	Marriage is no real excuse for not loving.
II.	He who is not jealous cannot love.
III.	No one can be bound by a double love.
IV.	It is well known that love is always increasing or decreasing.
V.	That which a lover takes against the will of his beloved has no relish.
VI.	Boys do not love until they arrive at the age of maturity.
VII.	When one lover dies, a widowhood of two years is required of the survivor.
VIII.	No one should be deprived of love without the very best of reasons.
IX.	No one can love unless he is impelled by the persuasion of love.
X.	Love is always a stranger in the home of avarice.
XI.	It is not proper to love any woman whom one would be ashamed to seek to marry.
XII.	A true lover does not desire to embrace in love anyone except his beloved.
XIII.	When made public love rarely endures.
XIV.	The easy attainment of love makes it of little value; difficulty of attainment makes it prized.
XV.	Every lover regularly turns pale in the presence of his beloved.
XVI.	When a lover suddenly catches sight of his beloved, his heart palpitates.

Andreas Capellanus, *The Art of Courtly Love*, trans. John Jay Parry. Copyright © 1941 by Columbia University Press. Reprinted with permission.

XVII.   A new love puts to flight an old one.
XVIII.   Good character alone makes any man worthy of love.
XIX.   If love diminishes, it quickly fails and rarely revives.
XX.   A man in love is always apprehensive.
XXI.   Real jealousy always increases the feeling of love.
XXII.   Jealousy, and therefore love, are increased when one suspects his beloved.
XXIII.   He whom the thought of love vexes eats and sleeps very little.
XXIV.   Every act of a lover ends in the thought of his beloved.
XXV.   A true lover considers nothing good except what he thinks will please his beloved.
XXVI.   Love can deny nothing to love.
XXVII.   A lover can never have enough of the solaces of his beloved.
XXVIII.   A slight presumption causes a lover to suspect his beloved.
XXIX.   A man who is vexed by too much passion usually does not love.
XXX.   A true lover is constantly and without intermission possessed by the thought of his beloved.
XXXI.   Nothing forbids one woman being loved by two men or one man by two women.

THE BUDDHA
FOUR NOBLE TRUTHS
6TH BCE

Four Noble Truths:

1. Life is Suffering.
2. Ignorance is the cause of Suffering.
3. The Cessation of Suffering which is the goal of life as it transcends pains and pleasure.
4. The Way to Cessation of Suffering is the Noble Eightfold Path which consists of:

   (1) Right Understanding
   (2) Right Thoughts
   (3) Right Speech
   (4) Right Action
   (5) Right Livelihood
   (6) Right Effort
   (7) Right Mindfulness
   (8) Right Concentration.

The Buddha said, "There are ten things considered good by all beings, and ten things evil. What are they? Three of them depend upon the body, four upon the mouth, and three upon the mind.

The three evil deeds depending upon the body are: killing, stealing and unchaste deeds. The four depending upon the mouth are: slandering, cursing, lying and flattery. The three depending upon the mind are: jealousy, hatred and ignorance. All these things are not in keeping with the Holy Way, and are therefore evil. When these evils are not done, they are ten good deeds."

Soyen Shaku, *Sermons of a Buddhist Abbot (Zen for Americans)*, trans. Daisetz Teitaro Suzuki. Copyright in the Public Domain.

CONFUCIUS
6TH BCE

THE DOCTRINE OF EQUILIBRIUM AND HARMONY

The heavens have conferred a human nature on mankind alone. Acting according to our humanity provides the true path through life. Wisdom from the past helps us learn how to follow this path.

It is wrong to leave this path for an instant. A path which you are free to leave is not the true path. On this account, the superior man is cautious and careful with respect to where he focuses his attention and how he is regarded; he is anxious to give his mind to only what is worth listening to and what is worth saying.

Secret thoughts and minute expressions of concealed feelings may be transparently obvious. Therefore the superior man is watchful over himself even when alone.

When there are no stirrings of pleasure, anger, sorrow, or joy, the mind may be said to be in a state of equilibrium. When those feelings are stirred and act in their due degree, there ensues what may be called a state of harmony. Equilibrium is the great root from which grow all acts of humanity; harmony is the universal path that guides them.

Let the states of equilibrium and harmony exist in perfection, and a happy order will prevail throughout the heavens and earth, and all things will be nourished and flourish.

Confucius, *Confucian Analects, The Great Learning, and The Doctrine of the Mean*, trans. James Legge. Copyright in the Public Domain.

THE SUPERIOR MAN

36. Tsze-lu asked what constituted the superior man. Confucius answered, "The cultivation of himself in reverential carefulness."

"And is this all?"

"He cultivates himself so as to give rest to others."

"And is this all?"

"He cultivates himself so as to give rest to all the people."

37. Confucius confessed, "The way of the superior man is threefold, but I am not equal to it. Virtuous, he is free from anxieties; wise, he is free from perplexities; bold, he is free from fear."

38. Tsze-kung also asked what constituted the superior man. Confucius replied, "He acts before he speaks, and afterwards speaks according to his actions."

39. "The superior man has nine things that are subjects of thoughtful consideration:

In regard to the use of his eyes, he is anxious to see clearly.

In regard to the use of his ears, he is anxious to hear distinctly.

In regard to his countenance, he is anxious that it should be benign.

In regard to his demeanor, he is anxious that it should be respectful.

In regard to his speech, he is anxious that it should be sincere.

In regard to his way of doing business, he is anxious that it should be reverently careful.

In regard to what he doubts about, he is anxious to question others.

When he is angry, he thinks of the difficulties his anger may involve him in.

When he sees gain to be got, he thinks of righteousness."

40. "The superior man wishes to be slow in his speech and earnest in his conduct. He is modest in his speech, but exceeds in his actions. In every action he considers righteousness to be essential. He performs it according to the rules of propriety. He executes it with humility. He completes it with sincerity. This is indeed the way of a superior man."

LAO TZU
4TH BCE

TAO TE CHING (DAOISM)

God (the great everlasting infinite First Cause from whom all things in heaven and earth proceed) can neither be defined nor named.

For the God which can be defined or named is but the Creator, the Great Mother of all those things of which our senses have cognisance.

Now he who would gain a knowledge of the nature and attributes of the nameless and undefinable God, must first set himself free from all earthly desires, for unless he can do this, he will be unable to penetrate the material veil which interposes between him and those spiritual conditions into which he would obtain an insight.

Yet the spiritual and the material, though known to us under different names, are similar in origin, and issue from the same source, and the same obscurity belongs to both, for deep indeed is the darkness which enshrouds the portals through which we have to pass, in order to gain a knowledge of these mysteries.

The Reason that can be reasoned is not the eternal Reason. The name that can be named is not the eternal Name. The Unnameable is of heaven and earth the beginning. The Nameable becomes of the ten thousand things the mother.

Therefore it is said:
"He who desireless is found
The spiritual of the world will sound.

> But he who by desire is bound
> Sees the mere shell of things around."

These two things are the same in source but different in name. Their sameness is called a mystery. Indeed, it is the mystery of mysteries. Of all spirituality it is the door.

LAO TZU QUOTES

Tao

The Tao that can be trodden is not the enduring and unchanging Tao. The name that can be named is not the enduring and unchanging name. (Conceived of as) having no name, it is the Originator of heaven and earth; (conceived of as) having a name, it is the Mother of all things.

The Sage

Therefore the sage manages affairs without doing anything, and conveys his instructions without the use of speech.

The Ruler

Therefore the sage, in the exercise of his government, empties their minds, fills their bellies, weakens their wills, and strengthens their bones. He constantly (tries to) keep them without knowledge and without desire, and where there are those who have knowledge, to keep them from presuming to act (on it). When there is this abstinence from action, good order is universal.

Emptiness

The Tao is (like) the emptiness of a vessel; and in our employment of it we must be on our guard against all fulness. How deep and unfathomable it is, as if it were the Honoured Ancestor of all things!

Tao and the Way of Water

The highest excellence is like (that of) water. The excellence of water appears in its benefiting all things, and in its occupying, without striving (to the contrary), the low place which all men dislike. Hence (its way) is near to (that of) the Dao.

The Female Mystery

The valley spirit dies not, aye the same;
The female mystery thus do we name.
Its gate, from which at first they issued forth,
Is called the root from which grew heaven and earth.
Long and unbroken does its power remain,
Used gently, and without the touch of pain.

SIMA QIAN

HAN DYNASTY
(2ND–1ST BCE)

HISTORY OF CHINA

Imperial Biographies: No. 12, Biography of the Filial Emperor Xiao-Wudi the Martial (r. 140–87 BC), translated by Ulrich Theobald

The emperor traveled, and then went eastwards, where he passed along and inspected the sea-coast. He made sacrifices and offerings to the Eight Spirits … In the fourth month, the emperor came back to Fenggao, where he thought about the words of the scholars and the magicians about the fengshan sacrifices for Heaven and Earth, that were all so confusing and misleading that is would be impossible to follow them. Thereupon the emperor went to the Liangfu summit to sacrifice the Lord of the Land, or Dizhu. On the day yimao, he ordered the official secretaries to wear their leather caps and the pinned official clothes and to perform the ritual shooting of oxen. In the east of Mount Tai, he had an altar erected for the Heavenly sacrifice that had to be performed like the sacrifice to the Great Unity in the suburbs. The altar was two zhang wide and nine zhang high, at the base of the altar a precious book-case was lying, but nobody knew what its content was. When the sacrifice was finished, the Son of Heaven alone with only a few secretaries and riding the carriage of (Huo) Zihou ascended Mount Tai to perform the feng sacrifice to Heaven once more. The performance of the sacrifice was thoroughly secret. On the next day he descended on the northern slope of the mountain. On the day bingchen, the emperor performed the chan sacrifice to the Earth at the north eastern corner of Mount Suran, like the sacrifice for the Mother Earth, or Houtu, is performed. All was performed by the emperor himself. We wore yellow clothes, and all ceremonies were accompanied by music … When the Son of Heaven came back from the fengshan sacrifices, he seated himself in the Clear Hall, where all ministers and officials wished him a long life.

SAMGUK SAGI: SOL KYEDU AND THE TEN INJUNCTIONS OF WANG KON

SAMGUK SAGI: SOL KYEDU 7TH CE

Sol Kyedu was descendant of a Silla official. Once he went drinking with his four friends, each of whom revealed his wishes. He said, "In Sill the bone rank is the key to employment. If one is not of the nobility, no matter what his talents, he cannot achieve a hight rank. I wish to travel west to China, display rare resources and perfect meritorious deeds, and thereby open a path to glory and splendor that I might wear the robes and sword of an official and serve closely the Song of Heaven."

In the fourth year, sinsa, of Wu-te (621 CE), Sol stealthily boarded an oceangoing ship and went to T'ang China.

THE TEN INJUNCTIONS OF WANG KON (KING T'AEJO) 10TH CE

1. The success of every great undertaking of our state depends upon the favor and protection of Buddha. Therefore, the temples of both the meditation and Doctrinal schools should be build and monks should be sent out to those temples to minister to Buddha. Late one, if villainous courtiers attain power and come to be influenced by the entreaties of bonzes, the temples of various schools will quarrel and struggle among themselves for gain. This ought to be prevented.

"Sôl Kyedu [From Samguk Sagi 47: 436]," *Sourcebook of Korean Civilization*, ed. Peter H. Lee, pp. 49. Copyright © 1993 by Columbia University Press. Reprinted with permission.
Selections from: "Koryŏ sa: The Ten Injunctions of Wang Kŏn (King T'aejo)," *Sourcebook of Korean Civilization*, ed. Peter H. Lee, trans. Hahm Pyong Choon, pp. 263–266. Copyright © 1993 by Columbia University Press. Reprinted with permission

3. In matters of royal succession, succession by the eldest legitimate royal issue should be the rule. But Yao of ancient China let Shun succeed him because his own son was unworthy. This was indeed putting the interest of the state ahead of one's personal feelings. Therefore, if the eldest son is not worthy of the crown, let the second eldest succeed to the throne. If the second eldest, too, is unworthy, choose the brother the people consider the best qualified for the throne.

5. I have achieved the great task of founding the dynasty with the help of the elements of mountain and river of our country. The Western Capital, Pyongyang, has elements of water in its favor and is the source of the terrestrial force of our country. It is thus the veritable center of dynastic enterprises for ten thousand generations. Therefore, make a royal visit to the Western Capital four times a year—in the second, fifth, eighth, and eleventh months—and reside there a total of more than one hundred days. By this means secure peace and prosperity.

PRINCE SHÔTOKU'S SEVENTEEN-ARTICLE CONSTITUTION
JAPAN 7TH CE

I. The Prince Imperial Shôtoku in person prepared laws for the kingdom: Harmony should be valued and quarrels should be avoided. Everyone has his biases, and few men are far-sighted. Therefore some disobey their lords and fathers and keep up feuds with their neighbors. But when the superiors are in harmony with each other and the inferiors are friendly, then affairs are discussed quietly and the right view of matters prevails.

II. The three treasures, which are Buddha, the (Buddhist) Law and the (Buddhist) Priesthood; should be given sincere reverence, for they are the final refuge of all living things. Few men are so bad that they cannot be taught their truth.

III. Do not fail to obey the commands of your Sovereign. He is like Heaven, which is above the Earth, and the vassal is like the Earth, which bears up Heaven. When Heaven and Earth are properly in place, the four seasons follow their course and all is well in Nature. But if the Earth attempts to take the place of Heaven, Heaven would simply fall in ruin. That is why the vassal listens when the lord speaks, and the inferior obeys when the superior acts. Consequently when you receive the commands of your Sovereign, do not fail to carry them out or ruin will be the natural result.

IV. The Ministers and officials of the state should make proper behavior their first principle, for if the superiors do not behave properly, the inferiors are disorderly; if inferiors behave improperly, offenses will naturally result. Therefore when lord and vassal behave with propriety, the distinctions of rank are not confused: when the people behave properly the Government will be in good order.

Prince Shôtoku, "Seventeen-Article Constitution," *Japan: Selected Readings*, ed. Hyman Kublin, pp. 31–34. Houghton Mifflin Harcourt Publishing Company, 1973.

V. Deal impartially with the legal complaints which are submitted to you. If the man who is to decide suits at law makes gain his motive, and hears cases with a view to receiving bribes, then the suits of the rich man will be like a stone flung into water, meeting no resistance, while the complaints of the poor will be like water thrown upon a stone. In these circumstances the poor man will not know where to go, nor will he behave as he should.

VI. Punish the evil and reward the good. This was the excellent rule of antiquity. Therefore do not hide the good qualities of others or fail to correct what is wrong when you see it. Flatterers and deceivers are a sharp weapon for the overthrow of the state, and a sharp sword for the destruction of the people. Men of this kind are never loyal to their lord, or to the people. All this is a source of serious civil disturbances.

VII. Every man has his own work. Do not let the spheres of duty be confused. When wise men are entrusted with office, the sound of praise arises. If corrupt men hold office, disasters and tumult multiply. In all things, whether great or small, find the right man and they will be well managed. Therefore the wise sovereigns of antiquity sought the man to fill the office, and not the office to suit the man. If this is done the state will be lasting and the realm will be free from danger.

VIII. Ministers and officials should attend the Court early in the morning and retire late, for the whole day is hardly enough for the accomplishment of state business. If one is late in attending Court, emergencies cannot be met; if officials retire early, the work cannot be completed.

IX. Good faith is the foundation of right. In everything let there be good faith, for if the lord and the vassal keep faith with one another, what cannot be accomplished? If the lord and the vassal do not keep faith with each other, everything will end in failure.

X. Let us control ourselves and not be resentful when others disagree with us, for all men have hearts and each heart has its own leanings. The right of others is our wrong, and our right is their wrong. We are not unquestionably sages, nor are they unquestionably fools. Both of us are simply ordinary men. How can anyone lay down a rule by which to distinguish right from wrong? For we are all wise sometimes and foolish at others. Therefore, though others give way to anger, let us on the contrary dread our own faults, and though we may think we alone are in the right, let us follow the majority and act like them.

XI. Know the difference between merit and demerit, and deal out to each its reward and punishment. In these days, reward does not always follow merit, or punishment follow crime. You high officials who have charge of public affairs, make it your business to give clear rewards and punishments.

XII. Do not let the local nobility levy taxes on the people. There cannot be two lords in a country; the people cannot have two masters. The sovereign is the sole master of the people of the whole realm, and the officials that he appoints are all his subjects. How can they presume to levy taxes on the people?

XIII. All people entrusted with office should attend equally to their duties. Their work may sometimes be interrupted due to illness or their being sent on missions. But whenever they are able to attend to business they should do so as if they knew what it was about and not obstruct public affairs on the grounds they are not personally familiar with them.

XIV. Do not be envious! For if we envy others, then they in turn will envy us. The evils of envy know no limit. If others surpass us in intelligence, we are not pleased; if they are more able, we are envious. But if we do not find wise men and sages, how shall the realm be governed?

XV. To subordinate private interests to the public good—that is the path of a vassal. Now if a man is influenced by private motives, he will be resentful, and if he is influenced by resentment he will fail to act harmoniously with others. If he fails to act harmoniously with others, the public interest will suffer. Resentment interferes with order and is subversive of law.

XVI. Employ the people in forced labor at seasonable times. This is an ancient and excellent rule. Employ them in the winter months when they are at leisure, but not from Spring to Autumn, when they are busy with agriculture or with the mulberry trees (the leaves of which are fed to silkworms). For if they do not attend to agriculture, what will there be to eat? If they do not attend to the mulberry trees, what will there be for clothing?

XVII. Decisions on important matters should not be made by one person alone. They should be discussed with many people. Small matters are of less consequence and it is unnecessary to consult a number of people. It is only in the case of important affairs, when there is a suspicion that they may miscarry, that one should consult with others, so as to arrive at the right conclusion.

Cao Vuong (Cao Bien)
Vietnamese Inscription
(870 CE)

Before he left An-nam, Kao P'ien ordered his bookkeepers to write down all that had been accomplished. The officials who supervised this program of public works further requested that their labors be commemorated with the erection of a stele. In 870, a tablet was set up in Kao P'ien's name with the following inscription:

Heaven and earth are boundless;
Man's strength is but a trifle.
Banish distress by bringing food;
Prosperity comes riding in boats.
Breaking free of this strange affairs,
Not just defeat but prolonged destruction,
I devised plans against civil disorder,
For excavating mountains and splitting rocks.
For meritoriously caring for those in need,
Thus rousing the power of thunderbolts,
Causing the sea to form a channel,
Where boats can pass in safety,
With the deep sea stretching out peacefully,
A highway of supply for our city.
The way of Heaven is the foundation of prosperity;
The majesty of the spirits supports and maintains

CPSIA information can be obtained
at www.ICGtesting.com
Printed in the USA
LVHW06s2015191018
594170LV00007B/18/P